Tales from the
1979 Pittsburgh Pirates
Remembering "The Fam-A-Lee"

John McCollister

www.SportsPublishingLLC.com

ISBN: 1-58261-838-0

Publishers: Peter L. Bannon and Joseph J. Bannon Sr.
Senior managing editor: Susan M. Moyer
Acquisitions editor: John Humenik
Developmental editor: Doug Hoepker and Kipp Wilfong
Art director: K. Jeffrey Higgerson
Dust jacket design: Kenneth J. O'Brien
Project manager: Kathryn R. Holleman
Imaging: Dustin Hubbart and Kenneth J. O'Brien
Photo editor: Erin Linden-Levy
Vice president of sales and marketing: Kevin King
Media and promotions managers: Mike Hagan (regional),
        Randy Fouts (national), Maurey Williamson (print)

Printed in the United States of America

Sports Publishing L.L.C.
804 North Neil Street
Champaign, IL 61820

Phone: 1-877-424-2665
Fax: 217-363-2073
Web site: www.SportsPublishingLLC.com

Dedicated to the memory of "Pops"

CONTENTS

FOREWORD

BY CHUCK TANNER

I MAY JUST BE THE LUCKIEST MAN who ever wore a baseball uniform.

Here I am, a native of the Greater Pittsburgh area, who not only had an opportunity to become a Major League Baseball player, but I am also one who has enjoyed the satisfaction of serving as manager of the Pittsburgh Pirates—a team I followed ever since I was a boy growing up in New Castle. As a big bonus, I had the opportunity to bring back to my hometown a World Series championship in 1979.

In this book you will read some of the stories about the people and events that made all of this possible.

Do you remember those monstrous shots into the upper decks at Three Rivers Stadium by Willie Stargell? Or the clutch pitching by Kent Tekulve, who dazzled opposing batters with his submarine pitch? And who could forget that song—that wonderful, glorious song; you cannot hear it without thinking of those battling Bucs of 1979 in their colorful uniforms.

As you read these accounts of our struggles, especially during the early part of the season, you'll notice one prevailing theme—nobody wanted that championship ring more than our guys.

No team ever won a World Series without a 15-game winner or a 100 RBI man. Willie Stargell was our leader, but I had 25 MVPs. We took a back seat to nobody. We were a "dirty shirt" ball club. We dared to dive headfirst into bases. We played run and hit. We weren't afraid to try anything. If we had just lain back, we wouldn't have played in, much less won, the World Series. It's as simple as that. We were a blue-collar team in a blue-collar town.

Other clubs may have had the best players. I had the best team.

In all my years in professional baseball, is there anything of which I am the proudest? I can answer that question with a profound "Yes!" It was that I was able to bring that trophy to my hometown. Not many managers can say that. You can say what you want, but Pittsburgh is a major-league city because of the Pirates.

May this volume bring back for you a heap of fond memories about a terrific team that represented the greatest city in America.

ACKNOWLEDGMENTS

THIS IS THE PAGE OF A BOOK that few people ever read. Normally, it's one in which an author thanks members of his family, everyone he used to date in high school and college, plus a rich relative whom he hopes will remember him in his will.

This fan of the Pittsburgh Pirates (who wears that designation with pride) may not go that far, but he is indebted to many people who made this book possible. They have gone above and beyond the call of duty in order to make this remembrance of the 1979 Fam-a-Lee a treat to write. To them, the author extends his sincere thanks.

One of these people is Chuck Tanner, who must rank among the most likeable men to have ever managed a team. This native of New Castle, Pennsylvania, with his trademark floppy hat and ear-to-ear grin, still radiates a contagious enthusiasm for the game and for the Bucs. He's a walking ambassador for baseball and for the Greater Pittsburgh region.

Two front-office people have left their marks on the team: former Pirate pitcher Nellie Briles, president of the Pittsburgh Pirates Alumni Association, and Ms. Sally O'Leary, who was a behind-the-scenes, "go-to" person ever since she began working in the team's public relations office and answering fan mail for the legendary Bob Prince. She is now editor of the Pirates alumni newsletter known as *The Black and Gold*. Both Nellie and Sally have contributed to the contents of this book.

Editors Kipp Wilfong, Doug Hoepker and the good people of Sports Publishing provided for this writer a most pleasant atmosphere and valued counsel.

Jim Trdinich and Dan Hart of the Pirates' media relations department have the unenviable task of supplying last-minute, on-the-spot data about Bucs past and present to newspaper reporters and broadcasters. Their continued cooperation in each of this author's ventures in writing books about the Buccos is applauded and appreciated, as is their valued friendship.

Pittsburgh Fox Sports Network supplied the author with videos of the remarkable '79 season and have been supportive in the completion of this project.

Fritz Huysman and sportswriters of the Pittsburgh *Post-Gazette* have lent their support in the research for this book.

Kevin McClatchy gets a standing ovation not only for the support of this writer in his various projects, but also for his dedication to the team and to the legacy of the Pirates. Those who know the history of the franchise can testify to the fact that he is the one man most responsible for keeping our team in the Steel City. In spite of the financial woes associated with a small-market team, McClatchy has brought competitive baseball to the area and has given us plenty of thrills. In addition, he and his staff have created for all Pirate fans the world's most beautiful ballpark.

Todd Miller, a Pittsburgh public relations and marketing consultant contributed research, fact-checking and editorial suggestions.

Finally, the author sends special thanks to the loyal fans of the Pittsburgh Pirates. Over the years, you have been faithful during times when others would fade away. Both players and management appreciate your dedication. Perhaps our greatest reward will be the day when, once again, we dance in the streets of the Golden Triangle and pop a cork or two in celebrating the coveted title as "City of Champions."

—JCM

INTRODUCTION

THE YEAR IS 1979 and America is in a funk.

Although President Jimmy Carter helped in negotiating international peace through the Camp David Accords less than a year earlier, most Americans remain unsure of his ability to provide strong leadership. Their suspicions are later confirmed with the kidnapping of 52 of their fellow countrymen by militant followers of an Iranian fanatic known as the Ayatollah Khomeini.

Double-digit inflation strikes us in our wallets; retail prices soar 13.3 percent, and interest rates approach an astronomical 20 percent.

You can buy a gallon of gasoline for 75 cents, but you sometimes have to wait in long lines at pumps due to some serious fuel shortages.

In Pittsburgh, anchors Bill Burns and his daughter, Patti, team behind the KDKA-TV news desk to bring us the gloomy reports about a near disaster at a little-known power-plant near Middletown, Pennsylvania, called "Three Mile Island," where a nuclear reactor came ever so close to a catastrophic meltdown.

Mayor Richard S. Caliguiri announces that a steady decline of business threatens to close the city's downtown department stores.

Headlines of the sports pages in the *Post-Gazette* and the *Pittsburgh Press* shock and sadden the baseball world when New York Yankees catcher Thurman Munson is killed in an accident in his private jet aircraft.

Movies of the year reflect an unmistakably somber theme. *Apocalypse Now* and *Kramer vs. Kramer* tell stories about various forms of depression and stress that seem to dominate our lives. Even popular songs such as "Heartache Tonight" lack the usual upbeat message expressed through music associated with previous generations.

If ever there is a time for relief, it's now.

Pittsburghers get some good news in January when their Steelers win Super Bowl XIII; they have every reason to expect the team to dominate professional football starting in September.

By far, however, the most refreshing breeze of optimism that sweeps over the Steel City this year is the performance of the 1979

Pirates. From the opening of spring training, the Bucs show promise for plenty of good days and nights at the ballpark.

Led by captain Willie "Pops" Stargell, along with flamboyant slugger Dave Parker, Phil "Scrap Iron" Garner, Tim Foli, and Mike Easler, the Bucs present an arsenal of solid hitters that creates a potent offense with the nickname "Lumber and Lightning." A balanced pitching staff with John Candelaria (14-9), Bert Blyleven (12-5), Bruce Kison (13-7), Jim Bibby (12-4), Grant Jackson (8-5) and Enrique Romo (10-5) keeps the Pirates in nearly every ballgame.

Often, string-bean, sidearm/submarine pitcher Kent Tekulve (10-8) is the deciding factor. The ace of the bullpen racks up 31 saves in an eye-opening, league-leading 94 appearances.

Called back to the team the previous year was catcher Manny Sanguillen, the popular native of Panama who had been swapped for manager Chuck Tanner. Now, the jovial Sanguillen accepts his role as a reliable backup to catchers Ed Ott and Steve Nicosia, and through timely hits and his upbeat personality helps mold 25 individual ballplayers into one cohesive unit.

Because of an impressive second-place finish the year before, just one and a half games out of first, and the squad's sheer determination throughout the '79 campaign, the Pirate faithful again have reason for hope. They buy bottles of champagne and pack them in ice as they witness their team edge closer and closer to winning it all.

Spurred on by 1,374,141 enthusiastic fans who attended home games at Three Rivers Stadium that year, and with the help of an adopted theme song recorded by the pop group known as Sister Sledge, "We Are Fam-a-Lee," the 1979 Pirates compiled an impressive 98-64 record, good enough for a first-place finish in the National League Eastern Division.

It wasn't easy by any stretch of the imagination. The dynamic Bucs got 25 high-drama wins in their last at-bat, and 51 of the contests were decided by one run. It was a cardiologist's nightmare. The race for the National League pennant was a dogfight until the last week of the season, with the Bucs finishing just two games ahead of runner-up Montreal.

The Pirates must face the Western Division-winning Cincinnati Reds in the National League Championship Series (NLCS). On paper, the Pirates are labeled as underdogs by many in the media. Nonetheless, the "Big Red Machine," with future Hall of Famers Joe

Morgan and Johnny Bench, prove to be no match for the Pirates, who sweep the best-of-five series three games to none.

"Bah!" sneer the experts, "Wait 'til they meet Baltimore in the World Series."

These caustic gurus have good cause to be skeptical. The powerful Baltimore Orioles, under the baton of scrappy manager Earl Weaver, are blessed with a stable of superstars. Sluggers Eddie Murray and Ken Singleton stand tall among other icons in a powerful offensive lineup. Pitcher Mike Flanagan leads the major leagues that year with 23 wins. It's no wonder that oddsmakers in Las Vegas consider the Birds from Baltimore to be heavy favorites to capture the World Series crown.

After four Series games, it seems all over but the shouting—for Baltimore fans, that is. The Bucs are down three games to one. Many critics expect the Pirates to throw in the towel and prepare for a long, cold winter. But Steel City fans, the manager, the players, the coaches and the local media simply won't allow that to happen. To the beat of "We Are Fam-a-Lee," the team known as "Chuck's Bucs" becomes the "Phoenix of baseball" and rises from the ashes. Baltimore fans can only watch in horror as the Pirates scratch and claw their way to win the final three games of the Series.

For the fifth time in their rich history, the 1979 Pittsburgh Pirates are champions of the world of major league baseball.

Willie Stargell richly deserves the Most Valuable Player (MVP) awards he receives for his performances in the NLCS and in the World Series; it is the first time anyone had won both awards during the same year. His regular-season record—.281 batting average, 32 homers and 82 RBIs—is enough to earn him a tie (with the St. Louis Cardinals' Keith Hernandez) for the National League's MVP Award. At age 39, he becomes the oldest player to win any of these honors.

More than a quarter-century later, Pirate fans still talk with childlike enthusiasm about their legendary '79 Bucs. None of the faithful ever hears a replay of the recording by Sister Sledge without thinking of Captain Willie and the magnificent Buccos who astounded the experts with their ability to overcome nearly impossible odds.

As a fitting tribute to the team and to its unquenchable spirit, today along Federal Street, in front of the world's most beautiful ballpark, stands a 12-foot statue of the late, great Stargell. Before or after each home game at PNC Park, many of those who were there during that '79 season pause near the base of that bronze replica of the powerful Pirate captain. They look with admiration at the bat held high and the imposing stare of the burly slugger peering out at a nervous pitcher who would rather have been waiting in a dentist's chair for a root canal without benefit of Novocaine. The more observant point to the statue's lower hand, only the thumb and three fingers of which grasp the bat. They all remember how the popular slugger twirled his bat like a windmill as he waited for the pitch. Their minds overflow with a legion of priceless memories of those smooth, potent swings and of the gargantuan homers that often followed. Most of all, they reflect upon that wonderful, magical season.

In the eyes of most is a glimmer of hope that says: "Perhaps . . . just perhaps . . . in my lifetime, I can see another championship flag fly over this ballpark."

When they leave the statue and mentally re-enter the real world of business and obligations, there's a renewed bounce to their steps. Some can be heard whistling, even singing the refrain to "We Are Fam-a-Lee."

And why not? To them this music is not merely an anthem of personal pride. It's a classic reminder of why baseball is the greatest game ever.

"We Are Fam-a-Lee!"

May that song never end.

—JCM

ONE REMARKABLE SEASON

To every thing there is a season, and a time to every purpose under the heaven.
        —Ecclesiastes 3:1

MANY PIRATE FANS TO THIS DAY recall, in vivid detail, the uphill struggle by the 1979 Bucs to win the National League East crown on the last day of the season. They remember also the ability of the Chuck Tanner-led squad in overcoming a favored Cincinnati Reds team in the National League Championship Series. They recreate in their minds and conversation the miracle finish of the World Series—beating a heavily favored Baltimore team that had Pittsburgh down three games to one.

As with championship teams of the past, the success of the '79 Bucs resulted from a combination of talent, skill, breaks and risks that paid off. However, there was one other intangible that other teams lacked: a prevailing spirit that enabled each player, coach and fan to celebrate life, not just as a baseball team representing a city; it was, instead, an honest-to-goodness Fam-a-Lee.

May the following recollections bring back for you a heap of fond memories from this fam-a-lee and help you to celebrate one of the great chapters in Pirates history.

A MOST COLORFUL TEAM

IF NOTHING ELSE, the Pirates of 1979 were the fashion plates of baseball. They donned an arsenal of uniforms that included yellow jerseys and white jerseys, yellow caps and black caps (both Cuban-style), yellow pants and black pants—enough for 64 possible combinations.

During the three seasons (1977-1979) that the Bucs wore these "bumble-bee" uniforms, reactions by the fans and media varied. Some applauded the innovative use of an extra splash of color and sparkle on the diamond. Others weren't quite so sure. Author and television commentator George Will offered a not-so-subtle reaction to these unusual combinations when he referred to them as "new forms of gaucherie."

HUMBLE BEGINNINGS

VETERAN CATCHER ED OTT vividly recalled the start of the 1979 season for the Pirates. "It was not very promising," he said.

Even in spring training the team was not performing up to expectations. Coming off a frustrating year in which the ball club narrowly missed winning the Eastern Division, the Bucs had to play on sub-par surface at McKechnie Field in Bradenton, Florida. "Field-wise, we fell down in the outfield and took out a divot that looked like a trash can lid," claimed the Pirates' number-one back-stop.

The first few weeks of the regular season showed little improvement. Like an airplane flying through a thunderstorm, the team was knocked around by the opposition. At the end of April, the Pirates were destined to be just another baseball squad with an unspectacular record of seven wins, 11 losses.

Pitcher Grant Jackson admitted, "We had a horrendous start. On the first of May we were six games under .500 and nine games out of first place."

"We'd always stunk coming out of spring training," remembered Ott. "But we were a veteran ball club and we knew what we had to do."

Although their bats came alive in May and the team began to win games, the Pirates were still six and a half games out of first place. The team still missed a piece of the puzzle if they were to become genuine contenders.

On June 28, they found that piece. The Bucs were in first place. Even though it was for only 24 hours, it felt mighty good.

THE MISSING PIECE OF THE PUZZLE

NOT OFTEN DOES THE ADDITION of one member to a baseball club make the difference between a pennant winner and an "also ran." But with the '79 Bucs, that was precisely the situation.

General manager Harding "Pete" Peterson displayed his genius when he acquired slick-fielding, power-hitting third baseman Bill Madlock from the San Francisco Giants. Coming to the Pirates, along with Lenny Randle and Dave Roberts in a trade for Eddie Whitson, Fred Breining and Al Holland, Madlock proved to be the sparkplug that got the Bucs firing on all cylinders.

"I think the whole thing that made the '79 team work was picking up Bill Madlock," said Ott. "He was the missing piece of the puzzle."

"After that," said pitcher Bruce Kison, "I felt that general manager Harding Peterson should get the 'Executive of the Year Award.'"

The facts support the claims of Ott and Kison. The Pirates were a 36-33 team before Madlock came on board; they went 62-31 after the trade. The Pirates accumulated more victories in that span of 93 games than did any other team that year in all of major league baseball. It was enough to propel them to the National League East pennant.

"Mad Dog" Bill Madlock was a key addition in '79.

VALUE OF THE MEN IN BLUE

LABOR MANAGEMENT PROBLEMS have disrupted baseball throughout its existence, and the Pittsburgh Pirates were in the thick of
things from the very outset. Bierbauer's, a popular hangout at PNC
Park, serves as a reminder of that fact for all Bucs fans. It's named
after the man who was chiefly responsible for the team name of
Pittsburgh's entry into major league baseball.

In 1889, through a clerical error, the name of infielder Louis
Bierbauer—one of the players who jumped from the Philadelphia
Athletics of the American Association (now the American League) to
the Philadelphia Brotherhood of the renegade Players League—was
inadvertently left off the list of those who were to return to their
original teams. As a result, J. Palmer O'Niel, president of the
Pittsburgh ball club—called the "Alleghenys" (the most often printed spelling at that time)—was quick to persuade Bierbauer to sign a
contract with his team.

The American Association cried "Foul!" O'Neil stood his
ground, insisting that Pittsburgh acted within the letter of the law. An
arbitrator's decision ruled that Pittsburgh did, indeed, have rightful
ownership of Bierbauer, so the newly signed contract was valid.

The American Association, frustrated in its attempts to win the
arbitration, responded with an emotional outburst: "The action of
the Pittsburgh Club is piratical."

The Pittsburgh team took some pride in that label. Both management and fans considered it as a badge of distinction. The name of
the club, as a result, was no longer the "Alleghenys"; from that day
forward, the team would forever be known as the "Pirates."

The 1979 major league baseball season began with another kind
of labor-management problem. This one involved not players, owners or leagues, but umpires. On March 7 arbiters from the National
and American Leagues walked out of spring training camps because
they had no contract, leaving the duties of calling balls and strikes to
minor league and amateur baseball umpires.

The strike continued into the regular season. The "replacement
umpires," however, missed far too many calls. "I really had a difficult
time knowing exactly where the strike zone would be on a particular day," remembers Pirate pitcher Rick Rhoden.

The lack of seasoned veterans behind the plate and working the bases demonstrated just how important it is to have nothing but the best on the field. Hence, the strike lasted just a few weeks before the umpires were called back.

WILLIE'S SECOND CHANCE

UNDERSCORING THE DIFFERENCE between full-time, professional major-league umpires and the so-called "replacement umpires" (the striking umpires publicly called them "scabs') was an incident that happened on Saturday, May 13, 1979. The Bucs trailed Cincinnati by a score of 2-1 in the bottom half of the seventh. With two men on base, Willie Stargell was called on by Chuck Tanner to pinch hit for reliever Jim Bibby. Reds reliever Frank Pastore got two quick strikes on the Pirate captain.

The next pitch was low and outside. Stargell started to swing, then stopped. Home plate umpire Bob Nelson ruled: "No swing." Reds manager John McNamara appealed. Nelson looked to third base umpire Harry Smail, who gave the "safe" sign, indicating that Stargell had checked his swing in time.

That brought McNamara from the dugout screaming in protest. As has been the case in nearly every similar argument over a century of major league baseball, the umpire held his ground.

Stargell, with renewed life at the plate, fouled off the next pitch, then drilled a sharp single to right, sending the tying run home. Omar Moreno followed with another base hit that brought home the go-ahead run that was enough to ensure the Pirates victory, 3-2.

After the game, the talk focused on the call by Umpire Smail. "It wasn't even close," said Pastore. "It was the most incompetent call I've ever seen in baseball." Manager McNamara agreed. "It was the most flagrantly miscalled play I've seen all year," he said.

Smail, a rotund, 350-pound-plus, fill-in arbiter had been the object of attention all week long. During the contest the evening before his infamous call, a fan rushed out of the stands and stole his cap, which was later retrieved and returned by the stadium police.

Smail never apologized for the apparent blunder that witnesses from both teams agreed was a wrong call. "In my judgment I felt he [Stargell] pulled back. He hadn't gone all the way through."

Stargell, the chief benefactor of the call, made light of the situation. Cincinnati's star second baseman and future Hall of Famer, Joe Morgan, recalled: "Willie jokingly said to me, 'How can he call me out, when last night I sent him two pizzas, a half gallon of beer and a hamburger on the side? Tomorrow, I'm going to send him a double order.'"

A MOST CONFUSING AFTERNOON

ON TUESDAY, JULY 24, 1979, during a Pirates-Reds game at Three Rivers Stadium, a fourth-inning call resulted in a 34-minute rhubarb. With Buc runners on the corners and a 3-1 count on batter Omar Moreno, Lee Lacy, who was on first, took off in an attempt to steal second. The pitch to Omar Moreno was called a ball, but Cincinnati catcher Johnny Bench instinctively threw to second ahead of the runner, Lacy. Lacy was called out by second-base umpire Dick Stello, even though Moreno has just received a walk (therefore entitling Lacy to second base). Lacy was not aware that Moreno walked, and he casually wandered off the bag.

Cincinnati second-sacker Dave Concepcion reached out with the ball and tagged Lacy, who was called out for a second time on one play. A heated argument followed, but Lacy was still out, according to the umpires.

The Pirates lost the game, 6-5, and filed an official protest with Charles "Chub" Feeney, president of the National League. The protest was rejected, and the Pirates' loss stood.

A GAME OF INCHES

ON SUNDAY, JUNE 5, 1979, Pirates pitcher Bruce Kison lost a no-hitter in the eighth inning against San Diego when the Padres' Barry

Evans, a .197 hitter, smacked a sharp ground ball down the third-base line that ticked off the outstretched glove of third baseman "Scrap Iron" Garner and went down the line for what the official scorer ruled a double, not an error. The partisan Pittsburgh fans groaned, but everybody in the stands knew it was clearly a hit. As the game panned out, it was the only hit Kison allowed all afternoon.

What many people may not know is that Kison was not scheduled to pitch that afternoon. He had pitched a scoreless inning in a 3-1 loss just 16 hours earlier during the previous game. Kison was so positive that he wasn't going to pitch that afternoon that he had eaten a sandwich just prior to game time. But Don Robinson, originally named as starting pitcher, experienced tightness in his shoulder during pregame warm-ups. Manager Chuck Tanner needed an instant starter. Kison volunteered. Bert Blyleven, Grant Jackson and Enrique Romo said they would be available once Kison grew tired.

Kison, however, never tired; Blyleven, Jackson and Romo never left the bench. Instead, all three joined the rest of the on-lookers who rooted for Kison during his masterful performance.

When Dave Winfield made the last out of the game, an enthusiastic crowd applauded and cheered the Pirate starter. Everyone was jubilant except one person—Bruce Kison. Instead of responding to the applause, Kison left the mound shaking his fist in the direction of the official scorer sitting in the press box.

Following the game, Kison was visibly disappointed at the ruling. In a desperate attempt to add a no-hitter to his impressive credentials that year, he used every emotional appeal in an attempt to convince the official scorer—writer Dan Donovan of the *Pittsburgh Press*—to change his call to an error. Donovan, however, stood his ground and refused to alter his ruling.

Later, after viewing replays of the hit, Kison accepted the decision. "I wanted it so bad," he said. "It's a once-in-a-lifetime opportunity. I came close, but no cigar."

Bruce Kison wasn't expecting to pitch on June 5, 1979, let alone come within a few inches of a possible no-hitter.

THE PIVOTAL GAME

WITH FEW EXCEPTIONS, a championship club can look back over its season and point to one game that made all the difference. For the 1979 Pirates that game took place on Saturday, August 11, at Veterans Stadium in Philadelphia.

During a nationally televised game with their cross-state rivals, the Pirates were being pummeled, 8-0, after only three innings. When the cameras panned the Bucs' dugout going into the fifth inning, even the most neophyte viewer could tell that the players felt they were in for a long afternoon. With heads hung low, many of them stared at their feet, hoping the game would end quickly and without much further embarrassment. It seemed that everybody knew it was a lost cause. Everybody, that is, except one person. Captain Willie Stargell.

"Pops" saw the discouraging looks on the faces of his teammates. In one of his rare outbursts of emotion, Stargell spoke pointedly to the players: "Quit your pouting," he demanded. "We're on national television. We can either kiss our butts goodbye or we can show everybody what the Pirates are made of."

To a man his teammates responded: "Let's do it!"

No motivational speaker could have done a better job. The Bucs chipped away. With one run here, two runs there, plus a lucky break or two, by the top half of the eighth, the Pirates were only two runs behind. With the bases loaded, catcher Ed Ott—a left-handed hitter—faced the Phillies' ace reliever, southpaw Tug McGraw. Ott looked back into the dugout thinking that Manager Tanner would surely send up a right-handed-hitting pinch hitter. "All I saw Tanner do," said Ott, "was clap his hands and shout at me, 'Go get 'em.'"

Ott obeyed. He smacked a hanging curve ball from the legendary McGraw high and deep. Left-fielder Greg Luzinski went back as far as he could go and helplessly watched the ball disappear into the right-center-field stands over the 371-foot mark. The grand slam put the Bucs ahead to stay. With 18 Bucco hits in the last five innings, the final score was Pittsburgh 14, Philadelphia 11.

"Suddenly," observed Pitcher Kent Tekulve, "all of the stars were aligned, and everything was clicking. That's when the club really decided, 'Hey, we've got something special here. This just isn't a regular baseball season. This is something special.' In short, from that moment onward, we refused to lose."

EPIDEMIC

"THERE'S AN EPIDEMIC on our ball club," said captain Willie Stargell. "The mouth is dry, and the stomach churns. But that's excitement, not pressure. It's the thrill that comes from being where we are."

Ed Ott's grand slam off Tug McGraw put the Pirates ahead for good on August 11. More importantly, it helped them turn the corner as a team.

Almost an "Oops!"

Sometimes strategies work out in spite of the percentages. Both manager Chuck Tanner and reliever Kent Tekulve can testify to that.

On Saturday, September 1, 1979, in the first game of a double-header, right-hander Tekulve was protecting a 5-3 lead in San Francisco. With one on and two out in the bottom half of the ninth, left-handed-hitting Darrell Evans was scheduled to bat. Since Evans, a consistent power hitter, could tie the game with one swing, Tanner played the percentages by calling in southpaw Grant Jackson to pitch to Evans. However, Tanner also wanted Tekulve to remain in the ballgame in the event Jackson could not retire Evans.

To keep his pitching options flexible, Tanner, whose strategies were sometimes both brilliant and bizarre, sent Tekulve to left field. The reason: if the pull-hitting Evans would make contact with the ball, most likely he would hit it to right or center field.

Evans did hit the ball, but instead sent a lazy fly to left field.

Tanner, watching from the dugout, cupped his hands over his eyes. He didn't want to watch.

Tekulve, profiting by the some sort of good fortune that seemed to follow the Pirates all year, happened to be standing in a perfect spot. As the fly ball came down, Tekulve barely had to move. Instead, he waved his arms frantically, as if to ward off any other outfielder from attempting to grab the ball. At the last second, he calmly raised his glove and watched the baseball as it landed in the pocket. Tekulve squeezed the horsehide to preserve the win.

After the game, Tekulve told reporters that they should not be surprised that a pitcher could catch a baseball. "Heck, during batting practice, all of us pitchers are out in the field shagging fly balls," he said.

Politically Incorrect

Three Rivers Stadium, home field for the '79 Bucs, had its share of both enthusiasts and critics.

Parking was one of the major complaints. The extreme difficulty getting in and out of parking lots around the stadium caused many fans to arrive home much later than expected. Also, the bowl-shaped facility contained too many seats for baseball, but not enough good ones close to the action.

Those who liked the facility when it was dedicated on July 16, 1970, appreciated its cleanliness as well as the expansiveness that gave any fan an unobstructed view of the diamond. The latter feature was a vast improvement over the many seats at the previous venue, Forbes Field, that were positioned behind steel beams supporting the second tier or roof.

Another difference noted by the fans was the improved lighting system. Some observers believed that Forbes Field had the worst illumination in all of major league baseball. The new lights at Three Rivers allowed both players and fans to enjoy a better view of the action.

Pirate management publicized parts of the stadium in a manner that, by today's standards, would be considered politically incorrect.

One of the two improvements trumpeted by the Pirates was the width of the stadium seats. Three Rivers' seats were 21" wide, three inches wider than those at Forbes Field. To demonstrate this advantage, the team endorsed a photo that appeared in an early 1970s edition of the *Post-Gazette*. It showed an obviously overweight man sitting in one of the new stadium seats. His head was tilted backward, and his eyes appeared to be closed. Under the photo was a caption that read: "An unidentified fat man tests the comfort of seats."

Another feature that undoubtedly would invite the wrath of those who are sensitive to such things in the modern era was a 274' by 30' electronic scoreboard above center field that featured unique graphics. Billed as "the first truly computer-operated scoreboard in the world," the scoreboard sometimes showed cartoons of young girls in miniskirts dancing around the word "Go." It was supposed to invite the fans to shout: "Go . . . Go. . . ."

Hometown fans, however, didn't catch the subtle reference to women as "objects" and "playthings," much to the chagrin of N.O.W. and similar organizations.

SOUR NOTE

NOT OFTEN DOES A STADIUM ORGANIST get headlines or letters of protest. But that's exactly what happened to Vince Lascheid, organist at Three Rivers Stadium during the '79 campaign.

Lascheid had become the focus of some mild objections when he tantalized opposing players with select renditions. One evening, when Ray Knight of the Reds struck out with the bases loaded, Lascheid played the music to "Silent Night."

Steve Garvey of the Los Angeles Dodgers, a handsome, clean-cut, All-American boy who could have had a career as a male model, strongly objected to Lascheid's playing of "There She Is, Miss America" as he stepped into the batter's box in Pittsburgh.

Receiving the most complaints was Mr. Lascheid's choice of songs when Cubs shortstop Ivan DeJesus bobbled a ball, allowing a Pirate runner to score. The organist chimed in with the popular hymn "What a Friend We Have in Jesus." The switchboard at Three Rivers lit up with protest calls, particularly from fundamentalist Christians, who thought the musical selection was borderline sacrilegious.

THE GAME THAT COUNTS

THE 1979 PIRATES showed little resemblance to a team on its way to a world championship in mid-May when they compiled a 12-18 record. But that would soon change. By winning 86 times over the next 133 games, they marched to an eventual National League Eastern Division title and, eventually, some World Series rings.

"That season taught me that anything can happen in this crazy game," manager Chuck Tanner said. "I've said this a million times— we may have had Willie Stargell and Dave Parker in our lineup, but we didn't have the best players. We did have the best team, and we proved that in the end.

"Our fans didn't quit on us that year, and they played a big part in us winning. We were all a family just like Sister Sledge sang about. We had one of the worst records in all of baseball after the first couple of months of the season, but then we got it going and we didn't stop until we won the last game of the season. And there's only one team that wins the last game of the season, and that's the team that gets to take home the hardware."

WHAT HAVE YOU DONE FOR ME TODAY?

SOME BASEBALL PLAYERS just can't do enough in the eyes of a few disgruntled fans. If you are a 6'5", vocal African-American, who is playing a kid's game, earning an annual wage 30 times the salary than most of the families in the stands, and was not in any way shy about wearing gaudy jewelry and (gasp!) earrings, that conviction increases. This attitude is especially true among those who have grown up with the "steel-mill mentality," which promotes the philosophy that the most honorable way to earn a living is by the sweat of your brow.

Some of the fans' dislike of Dave Parker became most apparent during a Sunday game at Three Rivers Stadium on June 24, 1979. The Pirate right fielder was in the midst of a solid year at the plate— batting .305, with 13 homers, 42 RBIs and 10 stolen bases. But because he was baseball's first million-dollar player, as good as he was, Parker was unable to please everyone with his performance on the field. He became the personification of the adage "The price of potential is the burden of expectation." As a result, while in Pittsburgh, Parker was subjected to loud booing by fans whenever he failed to live up to what they expected.

On this particular Sunday afternoon—a promotional game called "Bat Day" in which every child in attendance received a Little League bat—Parker further irritated the crowd by committing two errors in the field. It was a strange sight, indeed, to those who had seen this two-time Gold Glove winner make excellent catches and cut down daring base runners with spectacular throws.

One man from nearby Apollo expressed his displeasure by throwing one of the gift baseball bats onto the field in the direction of Parker, and the war club landed about 30 feet from where the Cobra was playing. Parker, who, a few years later, would be the target for another fan who threw a radio battery that barely missed his head, was told by a reporter that some people want nothing less than perfection.

"So do I," he said. "But we're all professionals, trying to do our best. No one is out there trying to make errors or make outs."

Parker did not mind the harsh words, but strongly objected to this particular fan's reaction. "You expect that on the road. I expect it in Philadelphia. My first thought was for my health. I am concerned about my livelihood. That was malicious. When you hear it was a grown man who threw the bat, you wonder what his intention is. If he can get mad enough to throw a bat on the field, you wonder what would happen if he had brought a gun along."

Jack Schrom, the Bucs' vice president for public relations, vowed that the team would press charges against the fan. "We want people to know that this sort of thing won't happen again," he said.

NOW, THAT'S CONFIDENCE

WHAT MADE THE '79 PIRATES so special? According to the Pirates' ace reliever, Kent Tekulve, there were two things—attitude and confidence.

As far as attitude, "It was a team that was unselfish and did not care about who the hero was, from top to bottom," he said.

There was also confidence that bordered on cockiness.

"We used to sit on the bench and we'd be down by a couple of runs in the sixth or seventh inning," said Kent Tekulve "we'd look over at the other team and start laughing at them. We'd say, 'Look at them, they think they're winning. They don't know we've already got three runs we haven't scored yet.' We knew we were going to come back."

THE TRADE EVERYONE SAID WAS WRONG

EVERY ONCE IN A WHILE, a general manager makes a trade that is denounced by the media as being unwise. And that was one of the more gracious comments.

Announcer Lanny Frattare remembers that on April 19, 1979, the Pirates had just arrived at the Shamrock Hilton in Houston to begin a series with the Astros. The Bucs were off to a lousy start, losing seven out of their first 11 games. Suddenly, the electricity in the hotel went off, which seemed like a commentary on the season so far. At that precise moment Manager Tanner called the players and some reporters up to his suite and, in the glow of candlelight, held an impromptu press conference. He announced that the Pirates' general manager, Harding "Pete" Peterson, had just traded shortstop Frank Taveras to the New York Mets for infielder Tim Foli and minor league pitcher Greg Field.

"Has Peterson gone mad?" asked one reporter. "This is just the kind of stupid trade that could ruin the Pirates' chances of winning the pennant."

The reporter's criticism, though harsh, was understandable. Taveras had been a steady and popular shortstop for the Bucs for eight seasons. In addition, he was a constant threat on the base paths, leading the league in 1977 with an eye-popping 70 stolen bases.

Foli, on the other hand, was rated by most clubs as an average hitter, an average fielder and an average runner. His "mark of distinction," if you could call it that, was his unpredictable temper. "He could go off on the deep end without a moment's notice," observed pitcher John Candelaria.

For a reason known only to the gods of baseball, somehow Foli's presence and aggressive personality helped to turn the team around. While the Pittsburgh club was 4-7 the day Foli put on a Pirates uniform, the team compiled a 94-57 record the rest of the way.

With his arrival in Pittsburgh, Foli changed not only as a player but also as a person. Perhaps it was the steadying influence of captain Willie Stargell or the patience of congenial manager Chuck Tanner. Whatever the reason, Foli became a total team player. "I knew that my challenge was to became a role player, and I was a set-up for the heavy hitters on the club," he said.

Foli's change of heart could well have resulted from an even deeper conviction—his religious faith. During that unforgettable '79 campaign, he became an outspoken representative of his Christianity. In fact, whenever he signed a photo from an admiring fan, he included a reference to one of his favorite verses from the New Testament.

Tim Foli wasn't gifted with long-ball power, as exhibited by his 25 home runs over a 16-year career. At the same time, he utilized his God-given talents and honed his ability to make contact with the ball. If he made an out, often it was what is known as a "productive out"—e.g., grounding out to the right side of the infield and advancing a runner, or hitting a sacrifice fly to score a timely run.

Tim Foli's value to the 1979 Championship club became most apparent when, in the World Series that year, he not only batted a respectable .333, he also made 33 appearances at the plate without striking out once. It's a World Series record that stands to this day.

Following the final out of the '79 Series, while the players popped champagne corks in the Pirates' locker room, not one of the media critics mentioned the "stupid trade that could ruin the Pirates' chances of winning the pennant."

A FOGGY DAY IN NEW YORK TOWN

THE SCORE WAS knotted at three runs apiece on the evening of May 25, 1979, at Shea Stadium in New York City. Outfielder Bill Robinson was stationed in left field during the home half of the 11th inning. The lights were bright. The temperature was cool. The wind was calm. There was only one slight problem. Robinson could not see the ball. In fact, he couldn't even see the pitcher and batter.

An eerie fog had crept into the stadium that made it impossible for anyone to see beyond 100 feet or so.

At the plate stood Mets outfielder Joel Youngblood.

Robinson heard the crack of a bat. Unbeknownst to him Youngblood had sent a fly ball to left. "Everybody was pointing and yelling at me," remembers Robinson. "At that moment all I could do is put up my hands and hope that I didn't get hit on the head." Fortunately for Robinson, the ball hit the sod 50 feet to his right. By the time the Pirate left-fielder retrieved the ball, Youngblood was standing on third with a triple.

Manager Chuck Tanner ran out of the dugout and screamed in protest to the umpire crew chief Billy Williams, who threw up his arms and called "Time." Play was halted for more than an hour. When conditions failed to improve, the game was called and went into the books as a 3-3 tie.

Joe Torre, manager of the Mets, may have argued the point, since his lead batter was on third with no outs. But the fair-minded Torre was perhaps thinking beyond the game when he told reporters, "Youngblood would not have been on third if it hadn't been for the fog. This is an act of God, and I'm not going to fool with that."

THE BEST CLUBHOUSE IN THE BUSINESS

IN THE BIBLE, the book of Proverbs says, "A merry heart does good like medicine." That adage might well have been applied to the 1979 Pirates. The atmosphere in the clubhouse often proved to be effective tonic for any hint of disharmony among the players and staff.

Dick Young of the *New York Daily News* was quoted by Jim O'Brien in a column for the *Pittsburgh Press*: "The best clubhouses to go into right now are the Pirates and Orioles. They treat you the best."

Others loved the Pirates' clubhouse, but for other reasons. Following a game, strains of the "We Are Fam-a-Lee" theme song filled the locker room. If the team had just won the game, it was an anthem of celebration. If the team lost, it was the beginning of a pep rally for next day's game.

Leading some of the sideshows in the clubhouse were slugger Dave Parker and scrappy Phil Garner. The two had a running battle of words throughout the season. Although there was not one ounce of animosity between them, the two delighted on engaging in a game of verbal "oneupmanship." To the delight of their teammates, the two seemed to plan their diatribes, sometimes peppered with obscene comments that would make a steelworker blush. Of course, when the game started, they both focused on the business of winning.

Pitcher Bert Blyleven was one who truly looked forward to showing up for work on any given day. "The clubhouse was like a zoo, and Chuck [Tanner] was the zoo keeper," he remembers. "Grown men acted like kids for six months. We couldn't wait to get to the ballpark just to see who was going to do what with whomever."

THE PIRATES' SECRET WEAPON

SOMETIMES PLAYERS USE the strangest gimmicks in order to win. For the '79 Bucs, a "secret weapon" of sorts was a handful of ... cabbage leaves.

Whenever the players had to endure the scorching heat of an August sun, team captain Willie Stargell introduced them to a rather effective, albeit crude, cooling ritual. Prior to the game, he showed the players how to wet down some cabbage leaves and stuff them inside their hats. Strange as it might seem, the tactic worked. The cabbage leaves kept the cool water inside the hats throughout the entire game. On occasion, however, this imaginative addition drew stares, especially whenever one of the Bucs raced home and slid hard into the opposing catcher, causing leaves of cabbage to fly out from under their hats onto the field of play.

Opposing managers and umpires often shook their heads in disbelief. Did any of them protest? No. At last report, there is no major-league rule that bans the use of cabbage leaves under baseball caps.

STARTING ALL-STAR

BIG DAVE PARKER of the Bucs earned the honor of representing the National League as a starter in the outfield for the 1979 All-Star Game on July 17 at the Seattle Kingdome.

Parker received 2,473,929 votes, second only to Dave Winfield of the Padres in votes cast for outfielders.

Joining Parker and Winfield as National League starters in the regular positions were Mike Schmidt (Philadelphia, third base), Larry Bowa (Philadelphia, shortstop), Davey Lopes (Los Angeles, second base), Steve Garvey (Los Angeles, first base), George Foster (Cincinnati, outfielder) and Ted Simmons (St. Louis, catcher).

The outspoken Parker made Pittsburghers mighty proud that evening. He went one for three in the 7-6 National League triumph. But it wasn't Parker's hitting that shone. Instead it was his defensive work, more particularly his throwing arm.

Parker made not just one, but two throws that became highlights of the game and were broadcast time and again by sportscasters in every major market.

The first peg came in the seventh inning. Boston's Jim Rice hit a high fly ball toward right that Parker lost in the lights. By the time Parker reached the ball that had fallen to the ground untouched, Rice had rounded second and was on his way to third. Parker turned and rifled a perfect throw to third. Rice was nailed. Even the partisan American League fans acknowledged the feat with a cheer.

The next inning, with two outs and Brian Downing of the Angels on second base, the Yankees' Greg Nettles sent a single to right that Parker corralled on a high hop. Downing rounded third and headed toward the plate. With a clothesline throw that National League manager Tommy Lasorda described as "a shot out of a cannon," Parker sent the ball on a line to catcher Gary Carter who blocked the plate and tagged out a hard-sliding Downing.

Following the game, Parker and his teammates headed for the showers. National League official Blake Cullen tapped Parker on the shoulder to inform him that he had just been awarded the MVP trophy for the game. "I was surprised," said Parker. "They had to practically drag me over to get the award." It was the first time in history that the All-Star Game MVP Award went to a player because of his defensive skills.

Parker credited his new fame to some of his fellow teammates. "Willie Stargell helped me with a lot of things, and when I was a young player, the late Roberto Clemente showed me a few things. We come from an organization where everybody passes things down to the younger players."

As a foretaste of coming attractions, Parker was somewhat over-whelmed by the pressure of the media following his splendid effort at the All-Star Game. "This is something new for me," he said. "I've done a lot of interviews, but the crowds are something." When a reporter reminded him that media crowds got worse when a team makes the playoffs and the World Series, Parker responded, "Well, I better get used to it, then, because that's where we're going to be."

CAUTION CITED BY THE COMMISSIONER

BOWIE KUHN HAD the enviable job as commissioner of baseball during the 1979 season. In the midst of the campaign, Commissioner Kuhn visited Pittsburgh. He recalled his earlier visits and issued a viable concern about the future of baseball.

"When I was a youngster, I used to visit my aunt who lived in Pittsburgh. My Aunt Helen and I would sit there on her porch lis-tening to Rosey Rowswell broadcast the Pirate ballgames. I remem-ber how Rowswell would signal a home run by somebody such as Ralph Kiner by crying aloud, "Raise the window, Aunt Minnie. Here she comes!"

At the same time, Kuhn showed increasing nervousness about another dimension of the game. He told a reporter for the *Pittsburgh Press*, "In general I'm concerned about the escalation of costs in our game, especially regarding player compensation. I think it's going up too fast," he said. "The average salary now is $125,000. That's fine. That means $3 million per major league team. That's fine, too. We can live with that. I wouldn't worry if it would stay that way for a while. It's the rate of escalation that troubles me.

"I don't begrudge the ballplayers more money, especially some-one like Dave Parker who may be the best player in the game today. I just don't want us to build ourselves into a deep hole."

Cousins

According to Pirate third baseman Bill Madlock, he and slugger Dave Parker are cousins.

"Not so," says Parker. "But we were pretty close. We got in trouble together."

Parker was referring to an incident in 1972 when the two of them played winter baseball in the Dominican Republic. "Bill wasn't hitting very good—about .125," says Parker. "And the fans were really on him. Bill made a gesture on the field. Right then and there they made up a new law that it was illegal to adjust your protective cup on the field. They do things like that, make new laws on the spot down there."

After the game, the police came to the team bus to arrest Madlock. "I figured I was hitting about .390, so I was all right," said Parker. "I told the police they had to take me, too." According to Parker, in the baseball-fanatical environment of the Dominican Republic, .125 hitters are much more susceptible to arrest than .390 hitters. "The bottom line is that I kept him out of jail."

In 1979, Bill Madlock and Dave Parker were reunited as teammates. Dan Donovan of the now-defunct *Pittsburgh Press* wrote, "Many times, that's closer than a cousin."

Go Where It's Safer

One of the athletes admired by Mike Easler of the Pirates was Sugar Ray Leonard, who had won the welterweight boxing championship in '79. That's not surprising once you consider the fact that the Cleveland-born Easler grew up in a household that encouraged him to participate in the sport.

"My dad wanted me to be a boxer, but I told him to take his gloves back and give them away," he said. "I wanted nothing to do with boxing."

Outfielder Bill Robinson was another Bucco who could have endorsed another sport. "I was the first black quarterback as a freshman at Elizabeth-Forward High," he told the *Pittsburgh Press*. "But one time I was running for a touchdown, and I got cut high and low by two guys near the goal line. They nearly killed me. I turned in my uniform the following day."

The Pittsburgh Pirates, especially during the drive for the pennant and the victorious World Series, were mighty happy that these two athletes chose baseball as their favorite sport.

JUST YOUR TYPICAL 75-CENT HOT DOG

WERE YOU TO ATTEND a game at Three Rivers Stadium during the championship season of 1979, here is the official price list for food and drink at the concession stands:

Hot Dog	$0.75
Hamburger	$0.90
Roast Beef	$1.50
"Big Buc"	$1.40
Super Dog	$1.10
Super Sub	$1.45
Sloppy Joe	$0.95
Small French Fries	$0.45
Large French Fries	$0.70
Pizza	$0.80
Pretzels	$0.35
Small Popcorn	$0.45
Large Popcorn	$1.00
Peanuts	$0.45
Ice Cream	$0.45
Small Soft Drinks	$0.45
Large Soft Drinks	$0.75
Coffee	$0.40
Small Local Draft Beer	$0.80
Large Local Draft Beer	$1.25
Local Cans	$0.85
Small Premium Draft	$1.00
Large Premium Draft	$1.40
Premium Cans	$1.00

CHAPTER TWO

THE UNFORGETTABLE SONG

Listen to that song and learn it! Half my kingdom would I give, As I live, if by such songs you would earn it!
—Henry W. Longfellow

CERTAIN SONGS ARE ASSOCIATED with memorable events and people. Listen to the refrain of "Auld Lang Syne" and you think of Guy Lombardo leading his "Royal Canadians" at a New Year's Eve party. The theme from Gone With the Wind brings back mental images of a dashing Rhett Butler and an ambitious Scarlett O'Hara. For fans of the 1979 Pirates, there was a disco song—"We Are Fam-a-Lee" as sung by a soul-disco quartet (later, a trio) known as Sister Sledge.

In more than 100 years of Major League Baseball, no one song has ever been as closely identified with one team. No one song has ever had so much influence on a team and on its fans. This pop tune became an anthem of inspiration and a battle cry that urged a group of scrappy players to perform better than they knew how.

The song did more than motivate the baseball team. It united an entire city. With the steel industry no longer a dominating factor in America's economy, local workers no longer enjoyed the luxury of job security. Two incomes were now necessary to maintain a household. Sons and daughters now left to seek their fortunes outside of the Greater Pittsburgh area.

Amid the doom and gloom came this song. This marvelous song. It became our "Theme from Rocky." It reminded us that we can overcome all the negative predictions about the future of the Tri-State area. It said that we can overcome anything that's been thrown against us in an attempt to check our advance.

The Pirates certainly benefited from that song and that conviction. Hence, the story of the 1979 Bucs is a testimony to the fact that, if you believe strongly enough in yourself, there is nothing . . . absolutely nothing . . . that lies beyond your grasp.

Not even a World Series ring.

THE SONG OF THE YEAR

ONE OF THE FACTORS uniting both the team and the Pirate fans was the popular song that contained the recurring theme: "We are Fam-a-Lee." Prior to games and during the seventh-inning stretches, spectators at Three Rivers Stadium—many of whom had never before met—held hands, swayed back and forth, and sang to the tops of their lungs the chorus: "We are Fam-a-Lee! We are Fam-a-Lee!" Even some of the Pirate players, many of whom could not carry a tune in a bucket, joined in. While this conglomeration may not have sounded like the Mormon Tabernacle Choir, it was enough to ignite a contagious enthusiasm that had been missing around Pittsburgh for far too many years.

Pitcher Kent Tekulve recalls, "We played that song in the clubhouse every game whether we won or lost. It reminded us that win or lose, we were still one big family."

"We didn't want to be sassy or fancy," said Willie Stargell. "It just sounded typical of our club. We had whites, blacks, Latinos, you name it. We had 25 guys united in achieving a common goal."

The city and the team became one. Both grew increasingly confident that nobody could overcome the "Fam-a-Lee."

NEARLY ANOTHER SONG

EVERY BUCCOS FAN knows that the theme song of the '79 Pirates was "We Are Fam-a-Lee." But did you know that another song nearly ended up being the song most identified with the team?

Slugger Dave Parker tells the story of how he was eager to cast his vote for another hit tune. Parker had become extremely fond of the words of the lively rendition of "Ain't No Stopping Us Now," which was a number-one R&B hit in 1979 for the Philadelphia duo McFadden and Whitehead. "I thought that reflected the hard-fighting spirit of our club," said the star outfielder who was known as the "Cobra."

That song could well have become the music identified with the Bucs that year had it not been for team captain Willie Stargell who was sitting in the Pirates' dugout listening intently to the strains of the famous rendition of Sister Sledge—"We Are Fam-a-Lee" as it was being played over the speaker system during a rain delay. Kent Tekulve tells of how Willie Stargell picked up the telephone in the dugout and called the press box, asking for Joe Safety, our director of publicity. Stargell said to Safety, "Announce to the crowd that this is the Pirates' official clubhouse song." Sure, enough, within minutes the announcement was made over the P.A. system.

Stargell's selection was endorsed by the rest of the club, even by Dave Parker. And the rest, as they say, is history.

THE SONG THAT GOT SOMEONE IN HOT WATER

GREG BROWN, now one of the play-by-play announcers for the Bucs, was an intern in the promotions department during the '79 season while attending Point Park College. One of his duties was to

If slugger Dave Parker had his way, the highlight reel of the '79 team would have been set to McFadden & Whitehead's "Ain't No Stoppin' Us Now."

play the music between innings at Three Rivers Stadium. That meant going out and purchasing 45 rpm records or albums that he deemed appropriate for play during a game.

When, for instance, Kent Tekulve would be summoned in from the bullpen, Brown played "Rubber Band Man" by the Spinners, and when Grant Jackson was in the game, he would play "Hit the Road, Jack."

During the season, he noticed that the Pirate players were playing in the clubhouse the disco song "We Are Fam-a-Lee." Brown then purchased a 45 record of the recording by Sister Sledge and informed his boss that he wanted to play this particular song during the game.

"No way!" said his boss.

Brown was disappointed, but he heeded the admonition of his superior.

About two days later, the Bucs made a spectacular come-from-behind win before a huge throng at Three Rivers. Caught up in the moment, Brown threw caution to the wind and cranked up the song over the P.A. system.

The crowd responded. "The place was rocking," recalls Brown.

Greg's boss was not exactly pleased with the young intern who disobeyed him. At the same time he could not help but realize that this was a genuine "happening." From that day forward, "We Are Fam-a-Lee" became the anthem not only in the Pirate locker room, but at Three Rivers Stadium as well.

ECHOES OF THE SONG

DALE PETROSKEY, a life-long fan and president of the National Baseball Hall of Fame and Museum in Cooperstown, New York, remembers, "Whenever that song was played, everybody in America thought of Willie Stargell and the Pittsburgh Pirates. It was their anthem. They showed everyone that it's possible to work together and have fun together and, if you believe in yourself, win together."

If you wish, you may sing along.

WE ARE FAM-A-LEE

• Artist: Sister Sledge
• LP/CD: We Are Family, Sony, 1979
• Composers: Nile Rodgers, Bernard Edwards

We are Fam-a-Lee
I got all my sisters with me
We are Fam-a-Lee
Get up everybody and sing

Everyone can see we're together
As we walk on by
And we flock just like birds of a feather
I won't tell no lie
All of the people around us they say
Can they be that close
Just let me state for the record
We're givin' love in a family dose

We are Fam-a-Lee
I got all my sisters with me
We are Fam-a-Lee
Get up everybody and sing

Livin' life is fun and we've just begun
To get our share of this world's delights
High hopes we have for the future
And our goal's in sight
No, we don't get depressed
Here's what we call our golden rule
Have faith in you and the things you do
You won't go wrong
This is our family jewel

We are Fam-a-Lee
I got all my sisters with me
We are Fam-a-Lee

Get up everybody and sing
Get up, get up, get up and sing it to me
Have faith in you and the things you do
Get up, get up, y'all
I got my sisters with me
We are Fam-a-Lee
I got all my sisters with me
We are Fam-a-Lee
I got all my sisters with me.

CHAPTER THREE

OUR BELOVED "POPS"

If you can keep your head when all about you are losing theirs ... you'll be a man, my son.

—Rudyard Kipling

WILLIE STARGELL
Age: 39 • Position: First Base

'79 Stats:

- Games: 126
- Home Runs: 32
- Batting Average: .281
- RBI: 82

HE WAS KNOWN BY SEVERAL NAMES. Some of his teammates called him "Captain." Sportscasters referred to him as the "soul of the team." Opposing pitchers knew him as "the team's slugger." Most of us, however, knew him simply as "Pops."

It was a name of endearment for someone who had won the hearts of young and old alike. No Pirate had worn that title before; certainly none will, as long as there's a sound of ash hitting horsehide.

In this unique Pirate Fam-a-Lee, there was no question about who was the head of the household. Wilver Dornel Stargell was the team leader who set an example of what it meant to be a big-league ballplayer. Sincerity was something that he brought with him to the big leagues.

Ever since this slugging first baseman/outfielder was signed by the Bucs as a free agent in 1958, this native of Earlsboro, Oklahoma, was on his way to establishing himself as a Pittsburgh icon. He earned that distinction based not only on his clutch hitting, but perhaps more importantly by the attitude he set for the club.

Catcher Ed Ott recalls, "When [Tim] Foli, I or others would come back to the dugout after striking out, we sometimes displayed our anger by slamming a bat into the bat rack. In fact, we went through quite a few bat racks that season. Not Willie. It wouldn't matter if he struck out six times in a row or just hit into a rally-killing double play, he always remained his same, cool self. He gently replaced his bat and returned to his seat on the bench, waiting to do his job the next time he stepped to the plate."

Willie Stargell was miles from the ordinary. He was the sole member in a club of one.

In 1988, Willie Stargell became the 200th member of Baseball's Hall of Fame in Cooperstown, New York. He was just the 17th player to be inducted in his first year of eligibility.

Prior to his untimely death in 2001, this 6' 2 1/2", 225-pound gentle giant dedicated much of his free time to waging war against sickle cell anemia.

GROWING UP FAST

WILLIE STARGELL'S EDUCATION into the real world—one filled with both glory and prejudice—came in the summer of 1959. The slender 18-year-old was playing baseball in Roswell, New Mexico, a

Pirates' farm team. It was not a very hospitable venue for a young African-American baseball player. Yet young Stargell had already caught the eyes of some scouts with his powerful hitting, slick fielding and all-out hustle on the diamond.

The real impact upon his life, however, came outside the stadium.

In Stargell's own words, "Two drunk cowboys stopped me at the ballpark. One jammed a shotgun in my face. 'Nigger, if you play today, I'm gonna blow your head off,' he sneered.

"Now, that got my attention. My knees shook. Yet for some unknown reason the man lowered the shotgun and just walked away.

"The ballpark was next to a highway. Later that afternoon, I don't know whether it was a truck or what, but I heard a tremendous 'Blam!' I thought I was dead. I actually wet my pants.

"I almost quit. But I'd call home and talk to my parents, and they'd say, 'OK. If you want to come home, do. But sometimes you have to put up with things to get somewhere.'

"I was miserable but I stuck it out. As the days rolled by I remained more and more determined that nobody . . . absolutely nobody . . . was going to stop me from making a living. I have to admit, however, that when someone threatens to blow your head off, a lot of things don't seem as important after something like that."

Willie Stargell experienced racism firsthand that afternoon, but he refused to let it be a distraction. "Hatred corrodes you," he said.

WHILE THE CAT'S AWAY. . .

AS IF THE BALTIMORE ORIOLES were not enough to worry about, while he was at Memorial Stadium struggling in a 5-4 loss during Game 1 of the World Series, Willie Stargell discovered more reason to feel bad. After he left the field, spoke with reporters and took a hot shower, the Pirate captain returned to his hotel suite only to discover that someone had broken into his room and robbed him of $2,000 in cash, some stereo equipment and some checks.

The thief, however, was not the sharpest crook in the criminal kingdom. In an attempt to get a few extra dollars, the man attempted to cash one of the checks at a hotel just three blocks down the street. In doing so, he showed the desk clerk his driver's license that gave, of course, his name and address.

Baltimore police had no problems tracing down the suspect.

THE MOTIVATOR

SEVERAL OTHER TIMES during the 1979 season, Willie Stargell was called upon to serve as the "Norman Vincent Peale of Baseball." He embodied the game by combining charisma with power. He showed his teammates how great the game can be. His influence extended beyond the white foul lines and into the clubhouse and dugout.

As a motivator he had few equals. Normally his counsel involved a few quiet words, one on one, with a struggling teammate. Stargell would take the distraught player aside and, in the privacy of a secluded corner of the locker room, place his giant hand on the shoulder of a younger player, look him eye to eye and speak pointedly with him about the situation. Nobody else heard what was said. Nobody else had to. Everyone knew that Willie was sharing with the youngster his experience and some solid tips on how to overcome any negative feelings he was having about himself.

Phil Garner called it a "quiet confidence."

That counsel was never more effective than on October 13 during the World Series. The Baltimore Orioles had just defeated the Pirates at Three Rivers Stadium when, before a disappointed partisan crowd of 50,883, the Orioles scored six runs in the top of the eighth that would be enough to defeat the Bucs by a score of 9-6. The Pirates were now down three games to one.

Stargell sat in the clubhouse with the losing pitcher that evening, Kent Tekulve, along with Phil Garner and Dave Parker. Without raising his voice, Willie laid it on the line: "We might lose this thing," he admitted, "but before we do, let's just show the world one time how the Buccos really play baseball."

They did just that.

THE STARGELL STARS

BOTH THE INSPIRATION as well as the solidifying element for the entire Pirate family on and off the field was Willie Stargell. "When Willie walked into the clubhouse," said Tim Foli, "everybody else stopped talking and waited for him to let us know what he had planned for that day."

Sometimes Stargell praised individual performances when, for example, he dispensed "Stargell Stars" to teammates who made exceptional plays or timely hits. The players, in turn, wore the golden stars proudly on their pillbox caps. It was this almost childlike incentive that helped bring fun back to the game of baseball.

"Willie not only praised us when his teammates did something outstanding," said Foli. When appropriate, he counseled a younger player who may be sulking about making a critical error about how they could best approach the upcoming game.

"You not only wanted to win, you wanted a 'Stargell Star,'" said Bert Blyleven.

In short, "Pops" and his Fam-a-Lee brought a refreshing approach to America's pastime when good news was needed the most.

LEADERSHIP

FOR THE FIRST ten years of his career, Willie Stargell was content to play in the shadows of the gregarious right fielder Roberto Clemente. Even though Stargell's production rate during the early '70s surpassed those by the native-born Puerto Rican known as "The Great One," Stargell was content to let his bat do the talking. Meanwhile, most of the reporters pressed in on Clemente—who was approaching a coveted 3,000-hit career—for an after-game quote.

Upon Roberto's untimely death on December 31, 1972, Willie Stargell reluctantly became the Pirates' leader. It was then that Stargell gave a quote with which he would be forever identified: "There's a time in a man's life when he has to decide if he's going to be a man."

If one of the signs of a great leader is that he does not allow his emotions to dominate his appearance, Willie Stargell was the master. While he enjoyed neck-and-neck encounters with great teams such as the Baltimore Orioles, he confessed that worrying about a forthcoming game often caused him to lose sleep and raised "goosebumps as big as quarters."

STARGELL, THE CUT-UP

WILLIE STARGELL WOULD never have been a threat to replace comedian Johnny Carson or serve as a guest host for *Saturday Night Live*, yet he displayed a sense of humor that often became a source of relief in the kind of tension that can build up within a ball club that must endure a 162-game season.

Pitcher Kent Tekulve recalled the time during the crucial Game 7 of the World Series when the Baltimore Orioles loaded the bases and were trying to rally. Up to the plate stepped slugger Eddie Murray. Tekulve pawed at the ground with his right foot, showing a bit more anxiety than normal.

First baseman Willie Stargell called "Time!" He walked over to the mound, reached down and picked up a fistful of dirt. He looked Tekulve in the eye and said with his deep, soothing voice: "If you're afraid of him, I'll pitch to him and you can play first."

For the first time in his major-league career, Tekulve laughed out loud while on the mound. A more relaxed Tekulve got the next pitch just where he wanted it—slightly high and over the inside corner of the plate. Murray swung and hit a lazy fly ball to right field. Dave Parker caught it, the inning was over and the Pirates eventually won the game, 4-1.

Sometimes with the opposition, Stargell was not afraid to psyche out a player with what might be dubbed a "whopper." Shortly before a night game at Three Rivers Stadium, Stargell convinced Cincinnati Reds shortstop Dave Concepcion that he would be ruled out if he touched a fielder while running the bases. That very night, Concepcion was so nervous about not making contact with Stargell, who was playing first base, that he momentarily lost his concentration and was easily picked off by Bucs pitcher Don Robinson.

WILLIE'S BIGGEST CHALLENGES

WILLIE STARGELL STRUCK an unusual pose while waiting for pitches. Instead of holding his bat steady (as taught by many coaches) this 6'2 1/2" mass of solid muscle struck fear into the hearts of opposing pitchers by swinging his 42-ounce bat in a windmill-like circle as if it were a toothpick. Then, at the very last fraction of a second, when the pitcher let loose of the ball, Stargell timed it so that his bat was held high (as shown on the statue outside PNC Park), and everything was set for his famous powerful swing.

However, Willie Stargell was not able to intimidate all National League pitchers. Three especially gave him a difficult time. They were the Cardinals' Bob Gibson, Steve Carlton of the Phillies and the Dodgers' Sandy Koufax. "Hitting against them," admitted Stargell, "is like drinking coffee with a fork."

GREATER LOVE HATH NO MAN ...

ONE OF THE OFT-QUOTED VERSES of the Bible reads: "Greater love hath no man than this, that he lay down his life for his friend." While Willie Stargell did not go quite that far, he came close, at least as far as Pirate announcer Steve Blass is concerned.

Blass was a teammate of Stargell's when the Bucs won the 1971 World Series. In fact, Blass was a star of that Series, pitching two complete games, including the never-to-be-forgotten 2-1 masterpiece for the final victory before a sellout crowd of disappointed Oriole fans in Baltimore.

But something happened less than two years later. Steve Blass could not seem to throw a strike. The man who used to dominate the opposition with pinpoint control, without any logical explanation just could not get the ball over the plate with any degree of regularity. Physically he was in great shape. The speed was there. The curve still broke sharply. His famous pitch called the "slop drop" looked the same. But Steve Blass could not hit the catcher's mitt. There was no explanation. Reporters who had never before witnessed anything like this happening, dubbed this phenomenon as "The Steve Blass Disease." During the period of this mysterious turn of events, "I felt very lonely," says Blass. "My teammates did not know what to say to me anymore. During batting practice when I pitched, nobody wanted to step into the cage, lest they get hit with a high, inside fastball."

Only one Pirate openly showed genuine support for Blass. That man was Willie Stargell. Blass remembers: "When it was my turn to pitch, Willie would always say, 'I'll be first.' He did it every time. He would go into the cage without a batting helmet. It was almost as if he was saying: 'Go ahead. Hit me in the shoulder. Hit me in the ribs. It doesn't matter. Our relationship is stronger than that.'"

THE STARGELL POWER

WILLIE STARGELL WAS in scoring position every time he stood in the batter's box; he embodied that much potential for hitting the ball out of the park.

"Nobody could hit a ball as far as Willie Stargell," said manager Chuck Tanner. "In 1979, in Montreal, he hit a ball so far there they painted the seat gold. I went up there the next day and sat in that seat, and everybody on the field looked like puppets, that's how far it traveled."

While playing for the Pirates' farm club in Asheville, North Carolina, Stargell was nicknamed "On the Hill Will" for the long homers he hit onto a hillside far beyond the right-field fence.

Even some players from opposing teams admired the power of Stargell. Hall of Fame second baseman-turned television broadcaster, Joe Morgan, said, "He hit some rockets at me. I remember one that he especially smoked. I dove for it and missed it. But that might have been a blessing in disguise. After Stargell reached base, our first baseman, Tony Perez, said to me, 'You know, Joe, if you had gotten your glove on that ball, it would have dragged you to death.'"

ABOUT AS HIGH AS YOU CAN GO

WILLIE STARGELL, one of the most feared sluggers in the game, at one point held the home-run distance record in almost half of the National League ballparks. For a long time, he was the only man who hit a ball out of Dodger Stadium—and he did that twice. In 1979, he hit a tape-measure homer in Montreal that went so far into the upper deck that they painted the seat gold in his honor. The shot was estimated at 535 feet! That an opposing club would do something to honor such an accomplishment is a testament to what Stargell brought to the game—a healthy respect.

A few years ago, when the Yankees traveled to Montreal for an inter-league game, during a lull in the action, MSG Network announcer Ken Singleton told the story of that prodigious homer. The camera panned up to the seat, where two shaggy young men, surrounded by a sea of empty seats, were conspicuously sharing a joint of marijuana. "I guess that's about as high as you can get!" announced Singleton.

THE TEAM'S "CRUTCH"

"WILLIE STARGELL WAS our team's 'crutch,'" recalled Bill Robinson, who batted ahead of Stargell in the lineup of the '79 Series. "Anything that you needed, any problems you had personally or in baseball, he took the burden.

"He was so easygoing. When I hit in front of him, I had the pleasure of hearing his gravelly voice saying, 'Get in that rocking chair, Big Bill.' I can remember asking him if I should take a pitch, and he would jump all over me. He'd say, 'Hit it like you live—hard.'

"Willie Stargell never did brag a whole lot, but he was most proud of a gargantuan home run he hit into the upper deck at

Veterans Stadium in Philadelphia. We'd come out of the tunnel before a game, and he'd look up there and point it out. He said it was still on the way up when it hit the seats and started rattling around."

MOST VALUABLE PLAYER OF THE WORLD SERIES

FOLLOWING HIS TEAM'S stunning upset of the heavily favored Baltimore Orioles, team captain Willie Stargell received an individual award—Series Most Valuable Player (MVP).

It was an awesome recognition for an awesome man, well deserved by the slugger whose .400 batting average and four home runs were greatly responsible for the Pirates' ultimate victory. His teammates agreed. Phil Garner—himself an MVP candidate who hit .500 and managed at least one hit in every game—said, "No better man could have won the award. Every time we needed a lift, he came through for us. And he never changed, whether we won or lost."

During the victory celebration in a locker room that was as jam-packed as the Fort Pitt Tunnels during rush hour, a champagne-soaked Stargell stood on a platform and was interviewed by reporters. One of them announced to Willie that he had just won the Series MVP Award. Stargell, in typical fashion, felt strange accepting the prize for himself. "I am proud to be the MVP," he said to a cheering crowd of media representatives. "I don't know what kind of award I'll receive, but I want it divided among our coaches, manager, clubhouse men and players. We needed all of them to win."

Willie Stargell was a remarkable human being, certainly. And he performed magic on the field. But whatever extraordinary powers Willie may have possessed, he could not fulfill the promise of dividing the MVP prize among so many people.

The prize was a brand new sports car.

WILLIE'S STATUE

ON FRIDAY, SEPTEMBER 29, 2000, Kevin McClatchy, managing general partner of the Bucs, announced at an afternoon news conference that a 12-foot statue of Willie Stargell would be unveiled at the club's new home, PNC Park, before the inaugural game.

Stargell sat with the 40,128 in the stands for that announcement prior to the final three-game set at Three Rivers Stadium that evening. He waved to the fans and openly wept.

Post-Gazette columnist Ron Cook wrote: "It's a wonder the old stadium didn't implode then, the ovation was so thunderous."

Serving as emcee that night was Stargell's former teammate and one of the Bucs' current broadcasters, Steve Blass. "They gave me a script to read," he recalled, "and I asked if I could add something to it. They said I could do so. After I read what I was supposed to read, I said, 'On a personal note, I'd like to say that when I was going through my problems late in my career, no one ever stood taller for me than Willie Stargell. Willie, I'll never forget that.'

"I'm so glad I said that now," says Blass.

After the ceremonies, Stargell approached Blass and gave him a giant hug. "What a hug!" Blass remembers. "Of course, there were no small hugs from Willie Stargell."

Although he was partially hidden by others surrounding his box seat, the fans could see the gentle giant openly weep. Pittsburgh wept with him.

Two nights later, on October 1, Stargell was at the final game, this time to step out onto the field in plain sight of everyone to throw out the honorary final pitch. What the fans saw that night sent shockwaves through the stands. Instead of the towering, 6' 2 1/2", 225-pound giant who had hit 475 soaring homers in his career and who hit more home runs (296) from 1970-1979 than anyone else in the majors, the Pirate faithful saw a man whose baseball shirt hung from his shoulders as though it were on a wire hanger. He was bent over like a man many years his senior. His once-thunderous voice was now reduced to a whisper. And that once-powerful throwing arm now lacked the strength to get the baseball from the pitching mound to the plate. Catcher Jason Kendall caught it on one bounce, but everybody present called it a "strike."

Stargell, however, did not live to see the day he would be forever immortalized at the statue unveiling on April 7, 2001. After not being able to attend the unveiling ceremony because of illness, the 61-year-old Hall of Famer passed away at New Hanover Regional Medical Center in Wilmington, North Carolina, from kidney failure in the early morning hours of April 9, the same day PNC Park officially opened its doors to begin a new era of Pirate baseball.

Stargell's bronze statue stands along Federal Street at the left field entrance to PNC Park. At the base of the statue is a quote from Stargell: "Last night, coming in from the airport, we came through the tunnel and the city opened up its arms and I felt at home." Adorning the base of the statue are "Stargell Stars," which, toward the conclusion of his 21-year playing career, the Pirate all-time home run leader gave teammates for their outstanding performances.

CONSEQUENCES

THE PIRATES COLLAPSED after Willie Stargell retired in 1982, and not just on the playing field. Outside problems, unfortunately, grabbed more headlines. A baseball-rocking drug scandal hit the sport following a 1985 federal trial in Pittsburgh that implicated more than 30 major league baseball players—including some Pirates.

In an attempt to win back some of the disgruntled fans in the Steel City, the Pirates coaxed the popular slugger out of retirement to become a coach under manager Chuck Tanner. When Tanner was let go by the Pirates and hired by the Atlanta Braves the next season, Stargell went with him.

While he was with the Braves, Stargell developed a kidney disorder that required periodic dialysis. His personal life also took another bitter turn when he divorced his wife, Dolores. In spite of these personal problems, he continued to work with the Braves' minor leaguers on their hitting techniques and approach to the game.

Willie Stargell's heart had remained always with the Pirates—the only major league team for which he played. Now sharing life with his new wife, Margaret, Stargell was elated when owner Kevin

McClatchy asked him to rejoin the Bucs in 1997, as an aide to general manager Cam Bonifay.

It was only fitting, therefore, that when he was inducted into Baseball's Hall of Fame in 1988, the plaque on the famous wall in Cooperstown pictures Willie Stargell wearing a Pirates cap.

WILLIE STARGELL QUOTES

"I love September, especially when we're in it."

ಐ

"I'm always amazed when a pitcher becomes angry at a hitter for hitting a home run off him. When I strike out, I don't get angry at the pitcher, I get angry at myself. I would think that if a pitcher threw up a home-run ball, he should be angry at himself."

ಐ

"It [the game] is supposed to be fun. The man says: 'Play ball,' not 'Work ball.' You only have a few years to play this game, and you can't play it if you're all tied up in knots."

ಐ

"They give you a round bat and they throw you a round ball. And they tell you to hit it square."

OTHER TRIBUTES TO WILLIE STARGELL

ON APRIL 9, 2001, when the news of Willie Stargell's death was aired throughout the nation, several major-league teams honored the Pittsburgh superstar with a moment of silence before their games; some even included a video montage on their electronic scoreboards.

What They Said About Willie Stargell

If, following your death, both your allies and your competitors sing your praises, you must have lived a good life. So it was with Wilver Dornel Stargell.

ဆ

"They loved him. White, black, Hispanic, it didn't matter. The love for Willie Stargell crossed all racial barriers in the clubhouse."

—*Milo Hamilton*
Former Pirates broadcaster

ဆ

"I will always remember Willie Stargell, the 21-year-old stud. He ran like a deer, had a cannon for an arm, and he could make the ball disappear. Willie Stargell was, and always will be, a Bucco."

—*Steve Blass*
Former teammate and current Pirate broadcaster at the memorial service for Willie Stargell at St. Mary of Mercy Church in Pittsburgh, April 17, 2001

ဆ

"The thing about him I'll remember most is how he could take all the guys, all different personalities, and simply bring them together."

—*Kent Tekulve*
Former Bucs pitcher

Our beloved "Pops." We'll never see his kind again.

ଚଠ

"He had dancing feet. He had the heart of a lion. He had
fun and he was funny. He was the strongest of men, the
greatest of heroes. Willie ... I'm hoping to
manage you again someday."

—*Chuck Tanner*
At the memorial service for Willie Stargell, April 17, 2001

ଚଠ

"Having Willie Stargell on your team was like having a
ten-carat diamond on your finger."

—*Chuck Tanner*

ଚଠ

"Willie Stargell was able to handle the highs and the lows
better than any man I have ever known. He wouldn't get too
high after a great game or too low if he struck out two or
three times. That rubbed off a little bit on me,
especially toward the end of my career."

—*Dave Giusti,*
Former Bucs pitcher

ଚଠ

"Willie Stargell didn't just hit pitchers. He took away
their dignity."

—*Don Sutton*
Hall of Fame pitcher, Los Angeles Dodgers

ଚଠ

"He was my hero. He's the reason I wore Number 8."

—*Joe Morgan*
Cincinnati Reds second baseman
and fellow Hall of Famer

ℬ

"We find it ironic that on one of the greatest days for the Pirate franchise—the opening of PNC Park—it's also one of the saddest. We lost a great player and a friend, but we still believe that his presence will be felt at the ballpark today. You can go back to the entire history of the organization and not find a player who was more of a Pirate than Willie Stargell."

—*Kevin McClatchy*

ℬ

"Time goes so fast. Why won't time stand still so we can still watch Willie play?"

—*Chuck Tanner*

ℬ

"He distributed T-shirts at Halloween and was a favorite among the neighborhood children. He mowed his own grass. That's how I remember him—as Willie Stargell the neighbor, not Willie Stargell the baseball player. He was an all-right guy. Fame never changed him."

—*Bernice Wheeler,*
neighbor in suburban Pittsburgh

ɞ

"Stargell was the patriarch of the great Pittsburgh teams. His influence was as imposing as his home runs. And his homers landed so far away plaques were put up to mark them. His build was imposing; he was almost frightening. The first time I asked him a question the inclination was to duck—or run. Instead, he was patient, understanding. His swings were devastating, but I don't think I ever saw him angry. The thing is, Willie Stargell hit a home run in life. It's still climbing, and let's hope it never ends."

—*Hal Bodley*
USA TODAY

ɞ

"Willie has earned his pedestal. He was a true leader in and out of uniform. I am proud to have passed his way."

—*Nellie Briles*

ɞ

"Perhaps the greatest compliment that I had given to Willie is that when my sons grow to be men, I hope they will be like Willie Stargell."

—*Phil Garner*

ɞ

"By the time Pittsburgh was in another World Series, Stargell owned the clubhouse, owned the town and had made a down payment on the nation's baseball public."

—*Paul White*
USA TODAY

ɞ

"Willie Stargell, one of the kindest, most intelligent, loveable persons, that despite his great ability, learned to respect and love people for what they are."

—*John Galbreath*

ଅଚ

"There are few people in this world who have the love and respect of all people like Willie. This man has been one of the best representatives that baseball has ever had."

—*Vernon Law*
Former Bucs pitcher

ଅଚ

"If there was a Hall of Fame for humanitarians, Willie Stargell would be a first-ballot Hall of Famer in that one, too. Come to think of it, I'm sure he made that Hall of Fame earlier this week."

—*Dale Petroskey*
President, National Baseball Hall of Fame and Museum

CHAPTER FOUR

THE PLAYERS

Baseball players are the weirdest of all. I think it's all that organ music.

—Peter Gent

FORMER NEW YORK YANKEES CATCHER Yogi Berra once said, "Good pitching will always beat good hitting and vice versa." Like so many things said by this legendary catcher, once you think of what's been said, it begins to make sense.

A good baseball club normally presents a blend of clutch hitting and solid pitching. The 1979 Bucs were no exception. With a team batting average of .264, the Pirates were able to push a league-leading 775 runs across the plate. The pitching staff posted a 3.41 ERA but was able to shut down opponents when needed as exhibited by the team's 52 saves—tops in the National League.

Along with Willie Stargell, the team captain, here are the others in the cast of characters on the '79 roster who made the entire city of Pittsburgh one happy fam-a-lee.

The Hitters

Matt Alexander
Age: 32 • Position: Outfielder

'79 Stats:
- Games: 44
- Stolen Bases: 13
- Batting Average: .538
- Runs: 16

Matthew Alexander's '79 statistics could be deceiving; during his 13 at-bats he scratched out seven hits, of which only one was of the extra-base variety (a triple). He saw limited action during the last four years of his big-league career with the Pirates (1978–1981) before he was sold to the Mexico City Tigers of the Mexican League.

Matt Alexander had amazing speed between the bases.

Alexander knew he was a role player and would never become a big-league star. However, his teammates appreciated his flying feet on the base paths that earned him the nickname of "Matt the Scat."

A relatively weak-hitting outfielder (a .214 average with no home runs over a nine-year career), this native of Shreveport, Louisiana, appeared in one game of the '79 series as a pinch-runner and defensive outfielder.

DALE BERRA
Age: 22 • Position: Infielder

'79 Stats:
- Games: 44
- Home Runs: 3
- Batting Average: .211
- RBI: 15

Dale Berra sometimes sounded a lot like his father.

LIVING IN THE SHADOW of a father such as Yogi Berra, who is both a Hall of Famer and an American icon, can't be the easiest thing in the world. Perhaps this is why Dale Anthony Berra had an unusually difficult time adjusting to the pressures of big-league baseball.

The Pirates' first-round selection in the 1975 draft was called up to the parent club just two years later. During the '79 season young Berra was a spot player, filling in when needed at shortstop and third base.

Three years later, Berra became the Bucs' regular shortstop. His problems with drugs contributed to the Pirates' decision to trade him to the New York Yankees in 1985, where he played just 16 games with his father as manager before Yogi was fired.

There was one thing that Dale did inherit from his father—a unique way of expressing a truth. Once, for example, he was quoted as saying, "You can't compare me to my father; our similarities are different."

MIKE EASLER
Age: 28 • Position: Outfield/Pinch Hitter
'79 Stats:
- Games: 55
- Home Runs: 2
- Batting Average: .278
- RBI: 11

THIS LEFT-HANDED-HITTING young man had a wealth of talent and literally feasted on minor-league pitching. In the majors, however, he was unable to show the same potency.

Mike Easler enjoyed his best year with the Pirates in 1980, hitting .338 with 21 HR and 74 RBI. With the '79 club, he was used as a pinch hitter and distinguished himself by collecting three hits in nine at-bats during the World Series.

In terms of his introduction and maturity Easler says, "I learned to love the game of baseball from my Dad; I learned to respect the game from Willie Stargell."

Mike Easler had many timely hits for the '79 Bucs.

TIM FOLI
Age: 28 • Position: Shortstop

'79 Stats:

- Games: 136
- Home Runs: 1
- Batting Average: .288
- RBI: 65

TIM FOLI WAS not the easiest guy to get along with. Over the nine seasons before the 1979 campaign, the six-foot, 179-pound shortstop had a well-earned reputation as a scrappy ballplayer not only on the field, but in the clubhouse as well. He was, in a sense, a "pop off" who openly criticized his own teammates and club management.

"Tim Foli could start a fight in a monastery," recalls one of his colleagues.

A decent hitter with a career .251 average, Foli enjoyed 16 years as a major leaguer, but none of those was as uplifting as his experience with the "Fam-a-Lee" in 1979. Shortly after his arrival in Pittsburgh two weeks into the season, Foli became a rock-solid shortstop who molded the infield. "I knew my role," said Foli. "I was not going to be an impact player but a role player."

While he was at the plate, coaches and base runners could count on Foli making contact with the ball, as exhibited by his 30 World Series at-bats during which he never once struck out. That was just one of the reasons why Manager Tanner called Tim Foli "the best second-place hitter I have ever seen in the big leagues."

During his three years with the Bucs, Foli added another dimension to his life—a strong religious faith. The radical change from the "Peck's bad-boy image" to the professing Christian surprised even his closest friends. He often accompanies his autographs with a reference to one of his favorite passages from the Bible—Romans 8:28. Today, Tim Foli is a popular speaker for youth rallies and at church services throughout the nation.

Since his retirement as an active player in 1985, Foli has served as a coach for several big-league teams.

NOW, THAT'S SHOWING 'EM

SHORTSTOP TIM FOLI had a well-earned reputation as being a "hothead" before he joined the Bucs in '79. His fights with other ballplayers and his record of flying off the handle at a moment's notice got him some uncomplimentary nicknames such as "Rubber Room" and "Crazy Horse."

If he became upset by the call of an umpire, Foli was at a disadvantage. If he yelled at an arbiter, he could get tossed out of the game; if he swung at one, it could mean a suspension or even a career-ender. Foli, then, used another kind of "revenge." If an umpire made a call that Foli did not appreciate during his first at-bat of a game, he would swing at the first pitch on each of his next trips to the plate so that the umpire would not have the opportunity to make another bad call.

BEST WORLD SERIES MEMORY

TIM FOLI'S BEST MEMORY of the 1979 World Series was in the eighth inning of Game 5 at Three Rivers Stadium. "Don Stanhouse was pitching, the bases were loaded, and I came to the plate. The fans started to chant: '*Fo-li. Fo-li. Fo-li.*'

"I had to step out of the batter's box to regain my composure," said the fiery shortstop. "Because I wasn't a superstar, I was not used to that. This meant a lot to me."

Foli rewarded the fans when he slapped a single, knocking in the final two runs in the 7–1 Bucco victory.

PHIL GARNER
Age: 30 • Position: Infielder

'79 Stats:
- Games: 150
- Home Runs: 11
- Batting Average: .293
- RBI: 59

PHIL GARNER WAS a gritty infielder who got by as much on determination as talent. His aggressive play drew the attention of Oakland A's manager Chuck Tanner in 1976. When Tanner moved to Pittsburgh the next year, he promptly traded for Garner (in a nine-player swap), who was used at third, then at second after the Pirates acquired Bill Madlock from the Giants on June 28, 1979. In 1978, Garner tied a major-league record with grand slams in consecutive games.

Garner was traded to Houston in mid-1981 for the younger Johnny Ray. In 1989, when his playing days were over following some rather "un-Garner-like" appearances with the Dodgers and Giants, Garner rejoined Houston as a coach. He later managed for eight seasons in Milwaukee (where he still holds the club record for the number of games managed and number of wins), in Detroit and in Houston.

SCRAP IRON

NICKNAMES HAVE BEEN associated with major league baseball players ever since the Cincinnati Red Stockings (the first professional team) donned spikes in 1869. Although the practice of dubbing players with odd-sounding names recently has become a lost art, the history of the game is peppered with names such as "Pee Wee," "Duke," and "Dizzy." The players became so identified with their nicknames that few fans, if any, would know that the real first names of these three Hall of Famers were actually "Harold," "Edwin," and "Jay."

An apt nickname given to the '79 Pirates second sacker, Phil Garner, was "Scrap Iron." It was a label given him by teammate Willie Stargell, who was impressed by Garner's tenacity. "He would dive and catch a ball by his teeth if he thought it was the only way to prevent a base hit," said the Pirate captain.

Phil Garner earned his nickname "Scrap Iron."

One local writer described Garner as "the best number-eight hitter in all of baseball." Manager Tanner told him, "You are my second clean-up hitter." Garner's .500 batting average in the World Series that year, with at least one hit in each of the seven games, underscored these claims.

LEE LACY
Age: 31 • Position: Outfielder

'79 Stats:
- Games: 84
- Home Runs: 5
- Batting Average: .247
- RBI: 15

WHEN YOU ARE BORN with a name like "Leondaus," you have to be tough. Lee Lacy was no exception. This scrappy Texan became an

With a name like "Leondaus," Lee Lacy had to be tough.

ideal utility outfielder during his first year with the Bucs in '79. He was quick, surehanded and had a potent throwing arm. He was also a dependable pinch-hitter as shown by his record of five pinch-hit homers, including a major-league record-tying three in a row the year before when he played for the Dodgers. The free-swinging, right-handed hitter came to Pittsburgh and batted .304 in his six seasons with the Pirates, with extensive starting time from 1982 to 1984, his final year in Pittsburgh, which included a National League-leading .996 fielding percentage.

BILL MADLOCK
Age: 28 • Position: Third Base

'79 Stats:
- Games: 154
- Home Runs: 14
- Batting Average: .298
- RBI: 85

"**WHEN THE CLUB** takes to the field," said manager Chuck Tanner, "Madlock takes charge." He was certainly instrumental in the Bucs winning the World Series.

Praises such as this notwithstanding, Bill "Mad Dog" Madlock may be the most overlooked four-time batting champion in the history of baseball. One reason is that he bounced among six teams in his 15 seasons.

Nobody could doubt his talent at the plate. With his short, compact swing, Madlock became the first major league baseball player to win more than one batting title with two different teams. He won the crown with the Chicago Cubs in 1975 and 1976, and with the Pirates in 1981 and 1983.

Bill Madlock, however, had a reputation not just for hitting baseballs. He was never afraid to engage in overt confrontations with opposing players, umpires, and even team owners. It was this last group of combatants who became a blessing for the Pirates.

In the spring of 1979, Madlock was playing third base for San Francisco. Giant management had already warned Madlock that they would no longer tolerate his outbursts that could embarrass the team. That warning was tested on June 26.

Atlanta Braves pitcher Bo McLaughlin threw a high, inside fast ball that sent Madlock into the dirt. After he regained his feet and dusted the red clay from his uniform, Madlock sent a harmless pop fly to the infield. While running down to first, he elbowed McLaughlin who was standing near the baseline. A full-scale baseball fight ensued. Giant management called this incident the "final straw." Two days later, they sent Madlock along with Len Randle to the Pirates in exchange for Ed Whitson, Al Holland, and Fred Breining.

WHATEVER IT TAKES

BECAUSE BILL MADLOCK had the reputation of being a hot-head, several players on the Pirates squad were concerned about how he would fit into their tight-knit Fam-a-Lee. "Don't worry about that," assured Dave Parker. "With Willie [Stargell] there to work with him, everything will be OK."

Several days after Madlock's arrival to the club, Manager Tanner took the opportunity to sit with him and explain that he could be asked to play at several positions. If Tanner expected him to rebel, he was, for one of the few times that year, mistaken. Madlock looked his manager squarely in the eye and said, "Skip, I'll do whatever you want me to do."

"I knew then that everything would be fine," said Tanner.

JOHN MILNER
Age: 29 • Position: Outfielder

'79 Stats:
- Games: 128
- Home Runs: 16
- Batting Average: .276
- RBI: 60

JOHN "THE HAMMER" Milner was a talented, left-handed-hitting outfielder/first baseman who came to the Pirates in 1978 with the potential to hit the long ball and to become a superb defensive player.

This native of Atlanta, who grew up a fan of Hank Aaron, adopted his idol's nickname; he even imitated his batting stance.

John Milner was called "The Hammer."

Throughout his career he showed flashes of greatness—especially as the regular first baseman for the National League champion New York Mets in 1973.

Milner played less for the Pirates, but in 1979 he contributed 16 HR (one of them a grand slam) in 326 at-bats while hitting a career-high .276. He was picked up by the Montreal Expos for their 1981 pennant drive. He returned to the Pirates in 1982, where he finished his career.

John Milner died in 2000.

OMAR MORENO
Age: 26 • Position: Outfield

'79 Stats:
- Games: 162
- Runs: 10
- Batting Average: .282
- Stolen Bases: 77

OMAR MORENO WAS born to be a center fielder. As a fleet-footed leadoff man for the 1979 world champion Pirates, he was an offensive and defensive threat. His uncanny speed in the outfield allowed him to reach a sharply hit ball before it found a gap, thus robbing opponents of extra-base hits.

At the plate, Moreno attempted too often to swing for the fences. As a result, the free-swinging Panamanian was a frequent strikeout victim. Hitting instructor Harry Walker convinced Moreno to chop down on the ball in 1979 (a strategy that's 180 degrees out of phase with what most coaches teach). As a result, Moreno hit a career-high .282.

His star shone brightest on the base paths. He led the league in steals in 1978 (71) and '79 (77), then set a Pirate record with 96 steals in 1980. He also led the league in triples (13) that year. He left Pittsburgh after 1982 as a free agent and thereafter bounced around the majors. He finished his career with 487 steals, 14th on the career list at the time.

A nickname given him by teammate Dave Parker, of course, was: "Omar the Tent Maker."

STEVE NICOSIA
Age: 23 • Position: Catcher

'79 Stats:
- Games: 70
- Home Runs: 4
- Batting Average: .288
- RBI: 13

DURING HIS FIRST full season in the majors (1979), Steve Nicosia was a platoon player. His proudest moment came when he was announced as the starting catcher for Game 7 of the Series.

The right-handed hitter exhibited decent offense as he batted .248 over an eight-year career (a bit more than five with the Bucs). After leaving the Pirates, he set a San Francisco record with eight consecutive hits in 1984.

ED OTT
Age: 27 • Position: Catcher

'79 Stats:
- Games: 117
- Home Runs: 7
- Batting Average: .273
- RBI: 51

ED OTT WAS nobody you would like to meet in a dark alley. This strong, rugged, 5'10" 190-pounder looked like a catcher, ran like a catcher and, most importantly, caught like a rough-and-tumble catcher. "The Otter" was a master at blocking the plate; for this reason his teammates nicknamed him "Troll"—after the mythical figure of fairy tales who blocked anyone from crossing his bridge. With a rifle-arm behind the plate, he once nailed seven runners in a row who attempted to steal second base.

A converted outfielder, he was Pittsburgh's starting catcher from 1977 to 1980, and batted an impressive .273 with 51 RBI in 1979.

On August 11 of that championship year, this dependable left-handed hitter once smacked a grand slam home run off Phillies reliever Tug McGraw as the Bucs won the game 14-11. It was the fourth grand slam that McGraw allowed that year, which tied him for first place on the all-time list with Ray Narleski of the Tigers.

After spending 1981 with the Angels, Ed Ott abruptly ended his playing career because of a torn rotator cuff.

This native of Muncy, Pennsylvania, loved the outdoors. Had he not been a baseball player, Ott says he would have been happy as a hunting guide.

Today he is a frequent guest on the Fox TV network and comments enthusiastically about his Fam-a-Lee of 1979.

WHAT'S IN A NAME?

IF PERCHANCE YOU are ever at a baseball game, someone might ask you: "Which major league baseball player has the shortest name (counting both first and last names)?" If you're a fan of the 1979 Pittsburgh Pirates, you should know the answer. Of course, it belongs to the Bucs' number-one catcher for that year, Ed Ott.

In that same vein, the big-league player with the longest full name was also a member of the Pirates in 1947 and 1948. He was a right-handed pitcher from Anadarko, Oklahoma, a seventh son, whose father named him after a United States president, a Roman emperor and an Indian chief. The pitcher's official name was: Calvin Coolidge Julius Caesar Tuskahoma McLish.

His teammates called him "Buster."

DAVE PARKER
Age: 28 • Position: Outfield

'79 Stats:
- Games: 158
- Home Runs: 25
- Batting Average: .310
- RBI: 94

DAVE PARKER HAD the unenvied challenge of replacing the legendary Roberto Clemente as the Pirates' right fielder. As Parker began to develop physically, he became an imposing batter, capable of hitting for power and average. His powerful right arm compared with Clemente's, and he won three Gold Glove Awards. That comparison was noted especially when, in 1978, he won his second straight National League batting crown—the first Buc to accomplish that feat since Clemente in '64 and '65.

In 1978, despite playing with a broken jaw, with a league-leading .334 batting average, 30 home runs and 20 stolen bases, Parker led the Bucs' second-half surge that fell just one and a half games short of catching the Phillies. That year he became the third Pirate to earn the league's Most Valuable Player Award (following the splendid performances of Dick Groat in 1960 and Roberto Clemente in 1966).

Knee and weight problems sapped much of his power in 1979 and 1980. Later it was discovered that drug problems might have contributed to his demise.

Owning a million-dollar contract, with even more dollars in deferred payments, Parker became a target for abuse in Pittsburgh. A hard-working father with a "steel-mill mentality" now had to spend more than an entire day's pay just to take his family to the ballgame. This same parent, who could recall the time he could see a Sunday doubleheader at Forbes Field for only a buck, protested the fact that so much money was given to a minority player (yes, racial prejudice still dominates the thinking of some baseball fans) whom he considered to be an arrogant braggart with an "in-your-face" attitude. As a result, Parker became for his hometown "fans" an object of boos, threats, even thrown objects.

Parker went to Cincinnati after the '83 season and retired as a player in 1991 after a 19-year career. In spring training, 2004, Parker and the Bucs put the past behind them when he was invited back into the Pirates' family as a hitting instructor.

As if to say: "We love you and beg your forgiveness," later that same year, when Dave Parker and other players from his former team were introduced to Pirate fans during the 25th Anniversary Reunion of the '79 Bucs at PNC Park, the Cobra received the most enthusiastic ovation.

In an ironic twist, some of the fans who chastised him during his playing career, now considered Dave Parker a candidate for baseball's Hall of Fame.

NOT EXACTLY ON THE ATKINS DIET

EARLY IN THE SEASON, the 6' 7" Dave Parker announced plans to become a vegetarian.

"What are you going to eat?" asked pitcher John Candelaria. "Redwoods?"

PITTSBURGH'S MILLION-DOLLAR MAN

IN 1979, DAVE PARKER became major league baseball's first million-dollar-a-year player. The Pirates did not particularly want to reveal this fact, lest some fans in the Pittsburgh area howl in protest that a baseball player earned that much money, while steel-mill workers had to count every penny just to afford a seat for a ballgame.

The Pirates, then, according to baseball statistics guru Bill James, hid a lot of the money in bonus clauses and delayed payments that were written in such a way that you almost had to be there when the contract was negotiated in order to know it was a million dollars a year. But it was.

BILL ROBINSON
Age: 36 • Position: Outfield

'79 Stats:
- Games: 148
- Home Runs: 24
- Batting Average: .264
- RBI: 75

BILL ROBINSON HAD a difficult time living up to his billing in 1967 when he came to the New York Yankees in his first full season in the majors, and manager Ralph Houk dubbed him as "the next Mickey Mantle." Unable to live up to that ballyhoo, he struggled with the media, the fans and himself while on the Yankees and Phillies. He nearly quit before finally maturing and hitting 25 homers in 1973.

With Pittsburgh, this native of nearby McKeesport never had one particular position. Manager Chuck Tanner employed the talents of the one he called his "super-regular" in the outfield, at first base, and at third base. In 1977, he reached career highs of .304, 26 HR, and 104 RBI. He hit 24 HR in 1979.

Following a short stint with Philadelphia, Robinson wrapped up his 16-year big-league career with a .258 average and 166 homers. He later served as a batting coach for the 1986 world champion New York Mets, and the 2003 world champion Florida Marlins.

Bill Robinson—only a few dared to call him "Blinky."

A PROPHET IS NOT WITHOUT HONOR, EXCEPT ...

STAN SAVRAN OF FOX SPORTS NEWS called Bill Robinson "the silent leader of the '79 Pirates." Savran explained that it was Robinson who showed a quiet strength when counseling with teammates and keeping the clubhouse on an even keel.

Robinson did not get that kind of respect from his immediate family. This man who grew up near Kennywood Park always knew when relatives were in the stands for a game at Three Rivers. They would shout at him by using a nickname used only among the family members. That name, which no outsider knew, was "Blinky." It was the result of a habit Robinson had as a child when he blinked during moments he became excited about something.

Please, however, if you ever see him, don't yell out the nickname. Even today, he's embarrassed about the nickname.

MANNY SANGUILLEN
Age: 35 • Position: Catcher

'79 Stats:
- Games: 56
- Home Runs: 0
- Batting Average: .230
- RBI: 4

MANUEL DEJESUS SANGUILLEN spent 12 of his 13 major-league years with Pittsburgh. The only exception was the one year (1977) he played for Oakland as a result of his memorable trade to the A's along with $100,000 so that the Pirates might acquire the services of manager Chuck Tanner.

If there was one thing that Manny Sanguillen lacked, however, it was patience while standing in the batter's box with his unorthodox batting style, holding his bat way over his head. During his 12-year span with the Bucs (1967-1976, 1978-1980), he seldom received a base on balls. In his eagerness to get hits, he swung at nearly anything close to the plate.

Former Bucs general manager Joe L. Brown once quipped, "I am convinced that whenever Manny gets a walk, either it's an intentional pass or paralysis has set in."

The jovial Panamanian was durable, catching more than 100 games in seven of his first eight full seasons with the Pirates. The exception was 1973, the season after his close friend, Roberto Clemente, was killed in an airplane crash; Sanguillen was chosen to replace Clemente in right field. The move did not work, and Sanguillen returned to catching. Following the popular Sanguillen's return to Pittsburgh in April 1978, he was relegated to the role as a reliable back-up to Ed Ott. He earned additional fame the next year when he hit a timely pinch-hit single to preserve a victory in Game 2 of the World Series.

He retired from baseball a year later. Today he is still a popular attraction for Pirate fans who see him running his barbecue stand at PNC Park.

LOYAL TO THE END

PERHAPS NO PLAYER of the 1979 Pirates was as devastated at the untimely death of Pirate legend Roberto Clemente as catcher Manny Sanguillen. In fact, Manny was one of the volunteer divers who searched for Clemente's body after the fatal plane crash on that New Year's Eve in 1972.

RENNIE STENNETT
Age: 28 • Position: Second Base

'79 Stats:
- Games: 108
- Home Runs: 0
- Batting Average: .238
- RBI: 24

PITTSBURGH'S RENALDO ANTONIO STENNETT, on September 16, 1975, was the first major-league player since 1892 to go seven for seven in a nine-inning game. His seven hits included two doubles and a triple while he scored five times. The bat Stennett used for this amazing feat is on permanent display in baseball's Hall of Fame.

With the Bucs since 1971, this strong-armed Panamanian was used frequently at shortstop and in the outfield before second baseman Dave Cash was traded to the Phillies prior to the 1974 campaign. Stennett loved his new position and responded by leading National League second basemen in both putouts and total chances per game (and did it again in 1976) while batting .291 and scoring 84 runs. He just missed Ken Hubbs's record of 418 consecutive errorless chances, falling short by eight.

This contact hitter had his best season in 1977, finishing second to teammate Dave Parker in the batting race with a .336 mark while stealing 28 bases, both personal highs. That season ended on a sour note, however, when Stennett fractured his right leg while sliding in a game against San Francisco, never hitting above .250 thereafter. However, he did tie a major-league record by hitting 1.000 as a pinch-hitter in the '79 Series (one for one).

Stennett was signed by San Francisco to a sizeable free agent contract following the championship season and finished his career in the City by the Bay in 1981.

JUST CALL ME "RENNIE"

FORMER PIRATE ANNOUNCER Bob Prince used to stick nicknames on certain players. Bill Virdon, for example, was "the Quail." Because of the way he uncurled at the plate while swinging at a pitch, Dave Parker was dubbed "Cobra." Since hard-throwing pitcher Ron Kline was from a small town in nearby Butler County, he was known as "The Callery, PA, Hummer."

To be baptized with a new nickname was a mark of honor among the Pirates. After all, Bob Prince did so only for favorites.

One of the '79 Bucs, however, did not eagerly accept his new moniker. Infielder Rennie Stennett, a frail-looking, sleek fielder, had just made a spectacular, diving grab of a line drive hit over second base for the final out of an inning. The native of Colon, Panama, immediately got to his feet and leaped high in celebration of the catch. Prince told his listening audience that Stennett, at that moment, looked like "The Gay Caballero."

Prince made several references to that designation over the next few days. When Stennett's teammates got wind of this, they poked fun at the youngster. Afterward, Stennett spoke privately with Prince in the locker room and pleaded, "Please, Mr. Prince, just call me 'Rennie.'"

FRANK TAVERAS
Age: 29 • Position: Shortstop

'79 Stats:
- Games: 164
- Home Runs: 1
- Batting Average: .262
- RBI: 34

FRANK TAVERAS PLAYED a significant role in the Pirates becoming the 1979 world champions. From 1974-1978, the volatile Taveras was the Bucs' regular shortstop. He hit .260 and drove in 140 runs during that span. On the base paths, he was no slouch as he broke Max Carey's Pirate record by stealing an National League-leading 70 bases in 1977. His 206 steals place him sixth in Pirate history. That was one of the reasons he earned himself the nickname "The Pittsburgh Stealer."

How did he help the Bucs win the World Series? Frank Taveras was the infielder traded during the early part of the '79 season to the New York Mets for Tim Foli—the man who became a key addition to the Pirates' infield that year.

THE PITCHERS

JIM BIBBY
Age: 34

'79 Stats:
- Games: 34
- ERA: 2.81
- Record : 12-4
- Innings Pitched: 137 ⅔

THE 6'5" 235-POUND Jim Bibby who was acquired by the Bucs as a free agent in 1978, pitched well for the '79 Pirates in both the

NLCS and the World Series. He came out of the bullpen to help keep the ship afloat after injuries racked the Bucs' starting rotation. As a starter during July and August, he came up with six straight wins and even smacked two long home runs. The next year, he was even better, according to many observers; his .760 winning percentage (19-6) was good enough to lead all other National League hurlers.

He was one of the three Pirate pitchers (John Candelaria and Dock Ellis were the others) who could boast of a major league no-hit, no-run game when, in 1973, while playing for Texas, he bested the Oakland A's, 6-0.

His finest game with the Bucs came on May 19, 1981, when his overwhelming fastball appeared to be more dazzling than usual. He allowed a leadoff single to Atlanta's Terry Harper, then retired 27

Reliever Jim Bibby stifled hitters with a blazing fastball.

Braves in a row. Shortly after that, Jim Bibby's career came to an abrupt halt due to a rotator cuff injury.

Following his playing days, Bibby coached 16 years in the minors for the Mets, Red Sox and Pirates before retiring because of double knee replacement surgery.

Bert Blyleven
Age: 28

'79 Stats:
- Games: 37
- ERA: 3.60

- Record: 12-5
- Innings Pitched: 237 ⅓

BERT BLYLEVEN (baptized Rik Albert Blyleven), a native of Holland, was the first pitcher born in that country to have any sort of a career in professional baseball. In his 1970 debut with the Minnesota Twins he was the youngest player in the majors and gave up a home run to the first batter he faced (the Senators' Lee Maye). He would eventually yield 430 gopher balls, including a major-league record 50 in 1986.

In the middle of his 22-year career, Blyleven came to the Pirates in December 1977 in a multi-team trade that brought John Milner from the New York Mets and sent Al Oliver and Nelson Norman to the Texas Rangers. In his first year with the Bucs, Blyleven made general manager Harding Peterson look like a genius when he led the club in ERA, strikeouts, starts, shutouts and complete games. Blyleven astounded his teammates and the fans with his "round-house" and "overhand drop" curve balls. Many, including Johnny Bench, Reggie Jackson and Rod Carew, called it the toughest break-ing pitch they ever faced.

A steady pitcher for the Bucs in 1979, Blyleven's star rose during the World Series in which he posted a 1.80 ERA in one start and a relief appearance.

His World Series record notwithstanding, Blyleven became increasingly unhappy with manager Chuck Tanner's strategy of sum-moning Kent Tekulve or Grant Jackson from the bullpen in close games. As a result, even though the durable Blyleven again led the team in innings pitched during the 1979 season, he notched only four complete games. Openly admitting his pursuit of statistical goals, a few weeks into the '79 season, Blyleven announced his intention to retire unless he was traded. The Pirates did not yield to his demand. Following the 1980 season, however, Blyleven was virtually given away to Cleveland in a six-player deal.

Bert Blyleven is a shoo-in: for the "Dutch Baseball Hall of Fame."

Blyleven's 287-250 career record puts him in the "iffy" category as a potential Hall of Fame inductee. Now a color commentator for the Minnesota Twins, the slender right-hander doesn't take this or himself so seriously. Even though he feels he is unlikely to be enshrined in Cooperstown, he quips, "I know I've got a lock on the Dutch Hall of Fame."

A LOYAL OPPOSITION

IF THERE IS ONE THING that pitchers hate more than a few missed calls by the home plate umpire, it's being yanked from a game when they feel they still have plenty of "stuff" left. Nobody was more vocal in his protest than Bucs right-hander Bert Blyleven.

Blyleven was in the middle of a respectable 22-year career during this championship season. He had posted some impressive numbers—a 12-5 record and a 3.60 ERA. However, on June 15, instead of celebrating his third victory of the season, the native of Zeist, Holland, suggested that Pirate management should trade him.

The Bucs had begun a three-game series against the Dodgers in "Tinseltown." Pittsburgh hung on to a 1-0 lead going into the bottom of the eighth. Blyleven, who had limited the Dodgers to only three hits, yielded a one-out single to Bill Russell. He then struck out Reggie Smith on a sharp breaking ball, but Russell managed to steal second on the pitch. Blyleven then tossed two hanging curveballs to slugger Steve Garvey that were out of the strike zone. On his own, Blyleven intentionally walked Garvey, thus putting the potential winning run on base.

To the mound strode manager Chuck "The Hook" Tanner, who called for ace reliever Kent Tekulve. Although Tekulve got the last out without allowing any damage and the Buccos scored five more runs in their half of the ninth, he did yield a two-run homer during the Dodgers' last at-bat, erasing the shutout.

Blyleven, whose one eye was lit up "Tilt" and the other "Free Game," was still livid following the game. "The two breaking balls to Garvey weren't great," he admitted, "but I still had my stuff. Who would you rather pitch to, Garvey with a two-ball count or to Cey? I'd rather pitch to Cey. The manager didn't like the walk, so he took me out."

Tanner disagreed. "I made the move because of the situation. You can't do things like that for any other reason. We've got Kent Tekulve on our team, who's one of the best relief pitchers in baseball. I went with my best."

Blyleven, who had always pitched in a four-man rotation, felt that he was a better pitcher on only three days' rest. He used this background to continue his tirade: "If I'm going to pitch every five or six days, get me out of Pittsburgh."

Tanner did not publicly criticize his pitcher's frustration. Instead, he employed the kind of diplomacy that prevents a feud between manager and player: "If I was the pitcher," he said, "I'd want the shutout and complete game, too. But I'm the manager, and I have to get the win for the team. I like Blyleven. I like his competitiveness."

JOHN CANDELARIA
Age: 25

'79 Stats:
- Games: 33
- ERA: 3.22
- Record: 14–9
- Innings Pitched: 207

JOHN "THE CANDY MAN" Candelaria has often been labeled as one of baseball's best "money" pitchers. From 1975 to 1988, he had only one losing season.

Candelaria became the focus of attention for several reasons on a special day at Three Rivers Stadium on August 9, 1976. First, he was named as starting pitcher for the 500th game played at the six-year-old stadium. Second, the game was aired on national television. Finally, the 6'7" southpaw with the unorthodox three-quarter-arm delivery gave fans even more reason to celebrate when he pitched a brilliant 2–0 shutout against the Los Angeles Dodgers, allowing but one walk while striking out seven. Most importantly, he allowed no hits. This native New Yorker with ties to Puerto Rico thus became the first Pirate ever to pitch a no-hit, no-run ballgame in Pittsburgh.

This wasn't a fluke by any means. During his 19-year career, John Candelaria controlled most of the games he pitched, striking out more than 100 batters in seven seasons (six with the Bucs).

John "Candy Man" Candelaria was a "money pitcher."

Candelaria's biggest asset was his outstanding control. He helped Pittsburgh win the National League East as a rookie in 1975 and set a NLCS record with 14 strikeouts in a losing cause in Game 3. Two years later he became the first National League pitcher since Sandy Koufax to win 20 games and lead the league in ERA (2.34) and winning percentage (.800). He was also Pittsburgh's first 20-game winner since Vernon Law did it in 1960 and the club's first left-hander to win 20 since Wilbur Cooper way back in 1924. He led the 1979 World Champions with 14 wins and pitched shutout ball in the crucial sixth game of the World Series.

Candelaria's toughest opponent, as it turned out, was injury. Plagued by chronic back and rib problems, Candelaria could sometimes be seen grimacing after a hard throw, but the gutsy southpaw never asked to be removed from a game. Despite his league-leading ERA, he was traded to California in August 1985, as the Pirates dumped their high-salaried players.

Candelaria wasn't through. He was the AL Comeback Player of the Year in 1986 and earned distinction as a relief pitcher for several other clubs, including the two teams—the Mets and Yankees—of his hometown. Following a two-year stint with the Los Angeles Dodgers, Candelaria finished his career by returning to Three Rivers Stadium for one last hurrah in 1993.

JOE COLEMAN
Age: 32

'79 Stats:
- Games: 15
- ERA: 5.18
- Record: 0-0
- Innings Pitched: 24 ⅓

JOE COLEMAN MAY have been one of the better pitchers in the history of baseball. Unfortunately, too few people know about him. With a record of 142-135 over a 15-year career in the big leagues, he twice won 20 games (1971 and 1973) and 19 games in 1972.

The crafty right-hander had his best years after the Washington Senators traded him to Detroit in an eight-player deal for Denny McLain in 1970. In Game 3 of the 1972 League Championship Series, he shut out Oakland 3-0, striking out an LCS-record 14 batters.

Coleman was briefly on the Bucs' staff during the 1979 season, appearing in just 10 games, his last appearances before retiring. Bucs manager Chuck Tanner did not include Coleman on the NLCS and World Series rosters, probably because his 6.10 ERA in 20.7 innings of work did not measure up to the performances of other pitchers who saw post-season action.

DOCK ELLIS
Age: 34

'79 Stats:
- Games: 20
- ERA: 5.77

- Record: 3-7
- Innings Pitched: 92

ALTHOUGH HE WAS not around for the NLCS or the World Series because he joined the '79 team on September 21, too late to be eligible for postseason play, flamboyant right-hander Dock Ellis was, and remains, one of the most colorful and controversial players among the cast of characters of the Pirates during the 1970s. Chief among his antics was anything that promoted his African-American heritage. He dressed in flashy clothes and often drew criticism from fellow players when he wore hair curlers in the locker room.

He was a rebel in other areas as well. He claimed that on June 12, 1970, he tossed a no-hitter in San Diego while under the influence of a hallucinogen.

At the All-Star Break in 1971, he was selected to start for the National League, but since Vida Blue was slated to be the starter for the American League, Ellis threatened to walk away from this honor, since, he said, baseball should never start "two soul brothers" against each other. Ellis and Blue eventually did start, and Ellis lost. He finished that world championship season with the Bucs while posting a career-high 19 wins. He was also the winning pitcher in Game 2 of the NLCS against the San Francisco Giants.

He wasn't through with controversy. On May 1, 1974, in what he claimed was an attempt to shake his teammates from complacency, he tied a major league record by hitting the first three Cincinnati batters he faced.

Ellis was traded to the New York Yankees in 1976 and enjoyed some flashes of success with several teams before returning to Pittsburgh at the tail end of the 1979 season—his last before retiring.

Dock Ellis wanted to be a Pirate until the end.

Although he knew he would not be eligible for postseason play, Ellis yielded to his heart. "I convinced [general manager] Pete Peterson that I wanted to die a Pirate," he said. "If this was going to be it, I could come back and fire them up in the clubhouse. That was my mission."

GRANT JACKSON
Age: 36

'79 Stats:
- Games: 72
- ERA: 2.96
- Innings Pitched: 82
- Record: 8-5
- Saves: 14

IN AN 18-YEAR CAREER marked by steep peaks and valleys, Grant "Buck" Jackson drew his greatest acclaim as a member of Pittsburgh's Fam-a-Lee in 1979. Jackson, who appeared in the '71 World Series as a member of the Baltimore Orioles, became the number-two man in the bullpen behind Kent Tekulve (giving the Bucs one of the finest right/left bullpen duos in the league), posting a career-high 14 saves. He finished third in the National League in appearances, behind teammates Tekulve and Enrique Romo.

Using a four-pitch repertoire of a fastball, slider, curveball and changeup, Jackson gave up no runs and only two hits in his six post-season appearances in '79. He was the winning pitcher in Game 1 of the NLCS and of the final game of the World Series which set off a post-Series celebration on the streets in downtown Pittsburgh and created a proud and lasting memory for Pirate fans everywhere.

Grant Jackson saved his best outings for the postseason.

Grant Jackson became the sixth African-American pitcher to win a game in a World Series.

BRUCE KISON
Age: 29

'79 Stats:
- Games: 33
- ERA: 3.19

- Record: 13-7
- Innings Pitched: 172 ⅔

PRIOR TO PERFORMING on the national stage of the World Series in 1979, Bruce Eugene "Buster" Kison had gained quick notoriety in the first night game in series history (1971) when as a rookie he entered Game 4 in the first inning with the Pirates already behind by three runs and got the final out. Over the next six innings his nervousness showed when he hit a Series-record three batters, but he allowed the Orioles only one hit to bring home a hard-earned 4-3 victory.

The slender, 6'4" 178-pound, baby-faced right-hander was the Pirates' 14th-round pick in the 1968 amateur draft.

Kison's status with the Bucs prior to the '79 season was questionable. During the previous campaign he was on the disabled list for 21 days due to surgery on the middle finger of his pitching hand. However, he was able to post a 5-4 record the rest of the way. He really came into his own in the drive for the pennant during the last part of the '79 season as he won his last five decisions.

Known for his willingness to pitch batters high and in tight, Kison (who won 13 games in '79) was the starting pitcher in Game 1 of the Series but lasted less than one inning when Baltimore scored a whopping five runs. It was his only appearance in this Fall Classic.

Following a nine-year stay with the Bucs (1971-1979), Kison moved on to the California Angels as a free agent before finishing his 15-year big-league career with the Red Sox with an impressive 115-88 record.

RICK RHODEN
Age: 26

'79 Stats:
- Games: 1
- ERA: 7.20

- Record: 0-1
- Innings Pitched: 5

RICK RHODEN OVERCAME childhood osteomyelitis (a bone disease). He wore a brace until he was 12 and had surgery to remove part of his left knee so it would not outgrow his right. An All-Star in his rookie 1976 season (12-3) with the Los Angeles Dodgers, he followed with a 16-10 mark. In April 1979 he was traded to Pittsburgh for Jerry Reuss and was disabled for all but one game.

He led the Pirates in wins in 1981 (nine), 1984 (14), and 1986 (15), and the Yankees in 1987 (16). An all-around athlete, he committed only six errors in his first 14 seasons. He was also a terrific-hitting pitcher and won three NL Silver Slugger awards for pitchers in 1984-86, compiling a .239 National League batting average.

Later Rhoden traded his baseball bat and glove for a driver and a pitching wedge.

He won his fifth Celebrity Golf Championship at Lake Tahoe in 1999 and is currently the top money winner on the Celebrity Golf tour.

DAVE ROBERTS
Age: 34

'79 Stats:
- Games: 47
- ERA: 2.90
- Innings Pitched: 80 ⅔

- Record: 5-4
- Saves: 4

ON JUNE 28, 1979, the Pirates completed one of the best trades in their history when they sent pitchers Ed Whitson, Al Holland and Fred Breining to the San Francisco Giants for southpaw pitcher Dave Roberts and infielders Bill Madlock and Lenny Randle.

Rick Rhoden is one person you would never bet against in a golf match.

Roberts changed organizations 11 times in his 13-year baseball career in which he compiled a modest 103-125 record—largely with cellar-dwelling teams. "The way I look at it," he said, "either I'm a bum or everybody wants me." Approached by 14 teams after graduating from high school, he was a Pirates farmhand before being taken by San Diego in the 1968 expansion draft.

From 1977 through 1981, he worked for six teams, never winning more than six games.

Roberts would be considered a good hitter for a pitcher; he had a career batting average of .194 with seven home runs.

DON ROBINSON
Age: 22

'79 Stats:

- Games: 29
- ERA: 3.87

- Record: 8-8
- Innings Pitched: 160 ⅔

HIS NICKNAME WAS "CAVEMAN." That was due primarily to his size and the way he clubbed a ball. Don Robinson was a hard-throwing, 6'4" 225-pounder who bounced back from elbow surgery to win *The Sporting News* Rookie Pitcher of the Year honors in 1978, when he went 14-6 for Pittsburgh. But he underwent shoulder operations in 1979 and 1981 before winning a club-high total of 15 games in 1982. His shoulder again kept him out for most of 1983, and he returned in 1984 as a relief pitcher.

The Bucs shipped Robinson to the San Francisco Giants in mid-1987, and he helped them win the National League West title.

QUITE A SLUGGER, TOO

AN EXCEPTIONAL FIELDER and hitter with home run power, pitcher Don Robinson played right field in the minors in 1983 when he wasn't on the mound. He was sometimes used by Chuck Tanner as a pinch hitter and for good reason. In his 15 seasons in the majors, Robinson posted a .231 batting average and smacked 13 home runs in his 631 trips to the plate.

ENRIQUE ROMO
Age: 31

'79 Stats:
- Games: 84
- ERA: 2.99
- Innings Pitched: 129 ⅓

- Record: 10-5
- Saves: 5

Enrique Romo used a sharp-breaking screwball to win games.

IN A RELATIVELY BRIEF six-year major league career, this bearded, fierce-looking reliever began his professional career as a teenager and pitched for 11 seasons in the Mexican League before going to Seattle in 1977. He became the Mariners' ace relief pitcher with 16 saves in '77 and 10 saves in '78.

This right-hander, who was in his first year with the Bucs during the '79 season, was noted for his sharp-breaking screwball. He kept the Pirates in the pennant race with a very respectable 10-5 record.

He appeared in two games of the '79 World Series and retired from the Pirates and from major league baseball following the 1982 season with a career 44-33 mark.

JIM ROOKER
Age: 36

'79 Stats:
- Games: 19
- ERA: 4.60

- Record: 4-7
- Innings Pitched: 103 ⅔

STARTING IN 1973, pitcher Jim Rooker spent the last eight seasons of a 13-year career with the Buccos. The sandy-haired southpaw came to Pittsburgh from Kansas City following the 1972 season, where he displayed not only talent with his arm but also prowess with a bat; he was the first player in Royals history, in fact, to homer twice in one game.

He racked up some fine years with the Pirates, winning 15 games in 1974 and again in 1976.

During the '79 Series, when he neared the end of his career, he held the Orioles to three hits and one run in five innings of Game 5.

Rooker moved to the Pirates' broadcasting booth and served as a color analyst with Lanny Frattare from 1981-1993. Perhaps his most famous broadcast came on June 8, 1989, when in Philadelphia the Bucs had a 10-0 lead in the first inning. Rooker announced, "If we lose this one, I'll walk back to Pittsburgh." When the final out was registered at Veterans Stadium, the Phillies won a wild game, 15-11.

Pitcher Jim Rooker gained distinction as both a Pirates announcer and "The Walking Man."

After the season, Rooker fulfilled his promise by walking the 305 miles in 13 days and raised $38,000 for charity.

KENT TEKULVE
Age: 32

'79 Stats:
- Games: 94
- ERA: 2.75
- Innings Pitched: 134 ⅓
- Record: 10-8
- Saves: 31

UNTIL JESSE OROSCO broke the record in 1999, Kenton Charles Tekulve was the all-time major-league leader in relief appearances with 1,050. He went 10-1 as a set-up man for Goose Gossage in 1977, and took over as the Pirates' closer after Gossage signed with the Yankees following the season.

With his sidearm/submarine delivery, the bespectacled, 6' 4", rail-thin Tekulve set a Pirates record in 1978 with 31 saves—a milestone he matched during the world championship year. He led the National League in appearances in both 1978 and 1979, setting a club record with 94 in 1979. That fall, he notched a World Series record of three saves, during which he struck out 10 Orioles in 9.1 innings.

Tekulve was the Pirates' all-time leader in saves (158) and was second to ElRoy Face in relief appearances (722) when he was traded to Philadelphia in 1985. In 1986, he broke Face's NL record of 846

How do you spell relief? "T-E-K-U-L-V-E."

trips from the bullpen. "Teke" became the first NL pitcher to have three 90-appearance seasons and, at age 40, became the oldest pitcher to lead the NL in appearances. Released by Philadelphia after 1988, he signed on with his hometown Cincinnati Reds. Midway through the season, with the Reds sinking in the standing he decided to retire from baseball.

Today this would-be schoolteacher (he graduated from Marietta College with a BA in Education), he is a tireless supporter of the Pirates and makes frequent appearances at PirateFest and other team-sponsored events.

TIMING IS EVERYTHING

IF YOU TOOK a side trip over to nearby Washington, Pennsylvania, in 2002, you possibly would have run into Kent Tekulve, one of the heroes of the '79 Bucs. He regularly worked with young players as operations director, pitching coach and first base coach for a baseball team known as the "Wild Things" of the independent Frontier League.

Tekulve, as much as anyone, could relate to the college-age players on this team who make little money and were never drafted, or had been released, by a big-league team. In reality, that's how his career began.

Tekulve, a graduate of tiny Marietta College in Ohio, was never thought to be a prospect worthy of a major-league draft. However, one eagle-eyed scout invited him to a tryout with the Pirates at Forbes Field on a summer morning in 1969. The 6'4", 155-pound Tekulve with the radical side-arm delivery stood out among the 100 or so other hopefuls on the field.

Tekulve was not invited back for the afternoon session. The reason: he was too slow of a runner.

"So what?" asked a puzzled Tekulve. "What has running speed got to do with pitching? What am I going to do? Steal home?"

The scout, however, insisted that the slim native of Cincinnati deserved a closer look. Yielding to the scout's plea, the Pirate coaches conducting the workout allowed Tekulve to return to the mound and pitch to one or two more hitters in the afternoon game. At that precise moment, Harding "Pete" Peterson, then the Pirates' farm director and later the general manager, walked onto the field. He had just learned that two pitchers at lower Class A Geneva were hurt, and there were no prospects in rookie ball ready to replace them.

"Good grief, they need two pitchers, and here I am getting ready to throw," Tekulve said. "I pitched my heart out. Apparently I looked better. This time, they were not concerned how fast I could run from home to first. That's how I got signed."

One of the things Tekulve found out during his time in the minors was that he was not a starting pitcher. He was most effective over a short period of time. A wise coach convinced him to become a reliever and, in five years, the submariner made it to the majors.

"Neither Kent Tekulve in the World Series, nor Kent Tekulve in Pittsburgh, would have never existed had I not made that afternoon game at that tryout," he said. "Success in life is often a matter of timing."

AN UPHILL CLIMB

ONCE HE FINALLY got the chance to play professional baseball, Kent Tekulve had a big hill to climb. Nobody in the Pirate organization thought that this pencil-thin right-hander would be an inning-eating starter. So, from day one, he was a relief pitcher.

"Anybody could look at my physical stature and know I wasn't big enough, wasn't strong enough, and wasn't capable of throwing seven, eight innings," he told Sally O'Leary, former mainstay in the Pirates' front office and now editor of The Black and Gold (the Bucs official alumni newspaper). Tekulve went on to explain, "It took me a long time—six and a half years—to get through the minor leagues because the innings didn't come as fast as a reliever as they did to a starter. But eventually you pitch in enough situations and all of a sudden when you walk out there and there's a man on second with two outs in the night inning in a one-run game, you've done this enough times that you're comfortable. You know what to do, and you just go do it."

ED WHITSON
Age: 24

'79 Stats:
- Games: 37
- ERA: 4.10
- Innings Pitched: 158

- Record: 7-11
- Saves: 1

DURING HIS FIRST full season in big-league baseball with the Pirates (1978), Ed Whitson was tagged as someone who could not miss as a starting pitcher. The big right-hander (6'3", 195 pounds) had all the credentials—a blazing fastball and sharp-breaking curve. Unfortunately he did not have a chance to get beyond the "promising prospect" stage as he posted a losing record with the Pirates.

But like Frank Taveras, his stay with the Bucs is best defined by a trade—this one on June 28, 1979—that brought third baseman Bill Madlock to the Pirates in what has been described as one of the best trades in the history of the franchise.

CHAPTER FIVE

THE MANAGEMENT TEAM

There are three things the average man thinks he can do better than anyone else: build a fire, run a hotel and manage a baseball team.

—Rocky Bridges

BASEBALL STRATEGY TODAY seems to be dictated by computerized statistics that tell a manager how a hitter has fared against a particular pitcher during a day game when the temperature is more than 72 degrees. It's not surprising, then, that in an era so caught up with micromanaging, major-league clubs now include a legion of coaches—one for pitching, another for hitting, one for the bullpen, and even one whose only job is to sit on the bench and whisper advice into the ear of the manager about what to do in particular situations.

Back in 1979, teams had a field manager (the term came from the early days of baseball when one person had to not only run a ballgame, but also arrange schedules, rooming assignments and other details now handled by a club's traveling secretary). Others on his staff would be a pitching coach, two base coaches, a trainer and a bullpen coach. That was it.

The responsibilities of the coaches varied depending on the club and its prevailing circumstances. Shouldering the blame for mistakes was the manager. As a result, if a team did poorly, the manager got fired. The philosophy, which still holds true today, was simple: It's easier to get rid of one manager than it is to transfer 25 players.

In 1979, managers of every team were faced with a new problem. Players were now one-season millionaires. The Pirate club that year was no exception as it became the first team to introduce a player (Dave Parker) into "The Seven-Figure Club"—one that used to be reserved for the nation's highest paid executives who oversaw the Fortune 500 companies. With players earning between five and ten times the salary of a manager, it was now the players who could dictate when they would play and how a team should operate. To make matters worse, top management of a baseball team often sided with the player over its field manager. Heaven forbid that the front office would make its million-dollar investment unhappy.

That was part of the genius of Chuck Tanner and his coaching staff. To handle 25 different personalities and egos, in an era when it was "cool" to rebel against authority, required the skills of a seasoned psychologist. To the delight of Pittsburghers, manager Chuck Tanner and his aides kept it all together.

This section is a salute to these remarkable souls who pulled the strings that converted a group of scrappy, individual ballplayers into a Fam-a-Lee.

CHUCK TANNER
MANAGER

A FAMILIAR SIGHT at every Pirates home game at PNC Park today is a smiling, suntanned man sitting behind home plate. Beneath his trademark floppy hat, the eyes of the seasoned "baseball lifer," who looks ten years younger than someone who's in his mid-70s, dart from side to side in an attempt to catch all of the action both on and off the field. If you watch him for more than a few minutes, you get the distinct feeling that he's seeing things that have gone unnoticed by you and everyone else in the park.

That spirited observer is none other than Charles William Tanner, a former major league outfielder and someone whose managerial success has made him a household name among baseball fans throughout the nation.

Chuck Tanner was a prime candidate for stardom in the Braves' farm system. From 1951 to 1954, he was one of the best outfielders in the history of the Atlanta Crackers of the Southern Association. The six-foot, left-handed-hitter racked up a .300 average in each of his four years with the Crackers. Tanner also excelled in the outfield. Under the watchful eye of manager and former big-league hurler Whitlow Wyatt (one of the best teachers he ever knew), Tanner helped lead the Crackers to the Class AA Grand Slam, winning the midseason All-Star game, pennant, postseason league playoff and Dixie Series over the Texas League champions. Tanner's excellent play earned him a promotion to the major leagues for the 1955 season.

In Tanner's first season with the Milwaukee Braves, he batted a respectable .247 and hit six homers in 97 games. His best season as a player was 1957, with the Braves and Cubs, when he batted .279 with 48 RBI. In 1958, his 53 pinch-hitting appearances led the National League.

During his eight-year career as a player for Milwaukee, the Cubs, Indians and Angels, he compiled a .261 batting average and hit 21 homers.

Tanner's real legacy in baseball would not be left on the diamond but inside the dugout. He learned the craft as a manager by serving eight seasons with minor league clubs. His big break came when he took the helm for the struggling Chicago White Sox for the last 16 games of the 1970 season. Immediately Tanner became popular with the fans and the media because of his infectious smile, good-natured personality, and never-ending optimism for baseball and for the chances of the Sox.

Manager Chuck Tanner often considered unorthodox strategies.

"People made light of my optimistic outlook," remembers Tanner, "such as: if I were captain of the Titanic, I would tell my passengers we were stopping for ice."

He eventually surprised even his staunchest supporters when he led the White Sox to end the 1972 season in second place and was given *The Sporting News* Major League Manager of the Year award. In baseball, as in other walks of life, however, fame is a fleeting thing. He was released by the front office just three years later following a fifth-place finish.

The next year, 1976, he managed the Oakland A's to a second-place finish and was considered by many, including the front office of the Pittsburgh Pirates, to be one of the premier managers of the game. With the retirement of longtime skipper Danny Murtaugh, the Bucs needed a seasoned veteran who could follow in the footsteps of this beloved, almost legendary Irishman. Through a series of unorthodox negotiations, Tanner was actually traded to the Pirates in exchange for catcher Manny Sanguillen and $100,000.

In 1977, he managed the Pirates to their highest victory total (96) since the World Championship 1971 season. In '78, his team mounted an unforgettable surge on the Eastern Division-leading Phillies, coming back from 11 1/2 games behind on August 12, clawing their way to a second-place finish in a pennant race that was not decided until the last day of the season. It's little wonder that Tanner was selected that year by the *Baseball Bulletin* as its Manager of the Year.

His most talked-about year, of course, was as head of the household of the fabled 1979 Fam-a-Lee, when his Buccos captured everything.

Tanner managed the Bucs from 1977-1985, during which time he amassed a 711-685 record. Pittsburgh released him after his squad finished in last place in 1984 and again in the cellar with 104 losses in 1985. Part of the reason for his firing was that the Galbreath family, the team's owners since 1946, sold the franchise to a group of local executives known as the Pittsburgh Associates.

As soon as it was known that Tanner was available, the Braves' Ted Turner quickly roped him in as his team's manager. But Tanner's positive outlook could not prevent his third straight last-place finish in 1986, nor his dismissal two years later after the Braves had gone 12-27. He enjoyed 17 consecutive full seasons as a manager—tops among active major-league skippers.

Tanner then directed his energies to supporting his ailing wife and raising his two sons, one of whom, Bruce, pitched ten games for the White Sox and A's and became the Bucs' bullpen coach in 2001.

Chuck Tanner needed every ounce of his positive spirit in October 2000. The then-71-year-old native of New Castle, Pennsylvania, had just gone to the Mayo Clinic for his routine annual check-up. "They told me, 'Man, you're perfect, you've got the body of a 50-year-old, there's only one problem. You've got prostate cancer,'" Tanner said. "I decided to get the treatments right away, and they really haven't bothered me at all. It's all in how you handle it mentally. They caught it in the early stages and they told me the recovery rate is between 90 and 95 percent."

Tanner drove 90 minutes each morning from his home in New Castle to Pittsburgh's Shadyside Hospital to be treated with the prescribed 40 external radiation treatments.

Today, to the delight of all Pirate fans and lovers of baseball, tests show no sign of that cancer reoccurring.

On Saturday, July 31, 2004, Tanner received another award. During the year of the 25th anniversary of the 1979 World Championship, Chuck, a graduate of Shenango High School in 1946 and "unofficial ambassador of Lawrence County," was honored with the dedication the high school baseball field at Shenango in his name. The field was named, appropriately, "Chuck Tanner Field."

"I was thrilled with the honor," said the former Bucs manager.

Chuck Tanner still resides in New Castle, where he raises thoroughbred horses and lends his name to a popular restaurant there. In New Castle, Chuck Tanner is "a man about town," except, of course, when there's a home game to attend at PNC Park.

NOT MUCH SECURITY HERE

CHUCK TANNER HAD no illusions about the mercenary nature of the baseball manager's occupation. "When I first became a manager," Tony La Russa once recalled, "I asked Chuck Tanner for advice. He told me, 'Always rent!'"

FLYING CHUCK

ON JULY 18, 1957, outfielder Chuck Tanner and a teammate, Hall of Famer Ernie Banks, created headlines when they both hit inside-the-park home runs at spacious Forbes Field, enabling the Cubs to win the game, 6–5.

ONE VERY STRANGE TRADE

WHEN HARDING "PETE" PETERSON assumed the duties as Pirate general manager in 1976 after Joe L. Brown retired for the first time (he would later be called back to the post nine years later), one of his first tasks was to acquire a manager for the team.

Fan favorite Danny Murtaugh had retired for the fourth time following the '76 season and was looking forward to spending time with his children and grandchildren. That dream was cut short just two months following his last game managing the Bucs. Murtaugh suffered a stroke and, two days later, on December 2, died at his home in Chester, Pennsylvania.

Finding someone to replace the man who had become a legend in the Steel City was not the most envied task. Peterson, however, had set his sights on former big-league outfielder Chuck Tanner.

There was only one problem, however. Tanner had just served one year of a two-year contract as manager of the Oakland A's. Since he was still under contract, Tanner could not just accept the Bucs' offer. Permission had to be granted by the shrewd, if not unpredictable owner—Charlie O. Finley. Finley insisted that he be compensated for losing his manager.

When Finley discussed this possibility with Tanner, he told him that the Pirates offered either All-Star catcher Manny Sanguillen or $100,000. "I'm going to demand both," he said.

Tanner recalls saying something to the effect: "They'll never give you that much."

In this instance, Finley demanded just that and, to the surprise of Tanner, Pittsburgh agreed to send both Sanguillen and a check for $100,000 to the A's in exchange for the popular manager.

It was one of the rare times in the history of major league base-ball that an active player was swapped for a manager.

A SPECIAL ANGEL

ON THE MORNING of Sunday, October 14, 1979, prior to Game 5 of the World Series, Chuck Tanner came to the Pirate clubhouse and, as was his daily custom, placed a telephone call to his mother who was in a nearby nursing home. It was a call he would never forget.

"I asked the nurse who answered the phone if I could speak with Anna Tanner."

"I'm sorry," said the nurse who did not know who was calling, "Mrs. Tanner just died."

A shock of such magnitude has caused players and managers in the past to succumb to grief and forget baseball for a while. Not Chuck Tanner. Calling upon an incredible amount of inner strength, he maintained his composure and led his club to three straight wins.

Pirate announcer Lanny Frattare recalled that he walked into the manager's office to extend his condolences. He asked Tanner if he felt able to lead the team that afternoon. Tanner assured him that he was more than up to that task. "My mother would want us to charge on," said the Bucs' skipper as he wiped away a tear. He then pointed to the heavens and added with a smile, "In fact, I am convinced that my mother went up there just to help us out a bit more."

"That," says Ed Ott, "in essence is what Chuck Tanner is all about."

Following Game 7, the triumphant Pirates flew home on the night of Thursday, October 17, amid the sounds of singing and pop-ping champagne corks. The next morning, most of the team was in New Castle at the funeral of Mrs. Anna Tanner.

A HALL OF FAME START

MANAGER CHUCK TANNER began his major-league career with a bang. In his initial at-bat as a rookie for the Milwaukee Braves, the 25-year-old Tanner was sent up to the plate as a pinch hitter on April 12, 1955. On the first big-league pitch he ever received, Tanner swung and clubbed a long home run off Cincinnati hurler Gerry Staley.

As it turned out, this may have been his greatest moment as a player. Tanner, who played until 1962, hit only 20 more homers. Ironically, the man for whom he batted—pitcher Warren Spahn— ended his illustrious career after hitting 14 more home runs than did Chuck Tanner.

Tanner's feat was tied 15 years later by a rookie catcher for the Detroit Tigers—Gene Lamont—who managed the Bucs from 1997-2000.

AN INSTANT REMEDY

CHUCK TANNER ASSUMED his first managerial assignment toward the end of the season for the 1970 Chicago White Sox. The team was short on talent, so he felt he needed all the help he could get to finish the season on a positive note. Tanner asked his predecessor, Don Gutteridge—a veteran who served 12 years as a big-league player and nearly two years as a manager—for any words of advice. The savvy Gutteridge slowly shook his head, smiled and told him, "Not really. I just left for you three numbered envelopes in the top drawer of the desk in the manager's office. When the team is in a slump and you don't know what to do, open the first envelope. If that doesn't work, open the second. If nothing changes, then fetch the third envelope."

That afternoon, Tanner went to the manager's office and, as Gutteridge had said, he saw the three numbered envelopes.

During the first few couple of games, the Sox continued with their losing ways. Tanner went to the desk drawer and pulled out envelope #1. Inside was a piece of paper with a simple message:

"Blame it on your predecessor." At the press conference that afternoon, Chuck Tanner did just that.

After another week of more losses and sloppy play, the pressure from the fans and media increased, he opened envelope #2. This one read: "Write a new lineup."

Tanner did that, too, albeit with little change in the outcome of the games. Finally, the rumblings in the newspapers became more intense. Following his not-so-impressive record of only three wins and 13 losses, Tanner read a comment in the morning newspaper by one columnist who suggested another change in managers. Tanner quickly ran to the desk and opened envelope #3. The message was written in bold print: "Prepare three envelopes."

HOW TOUGH IS IT TO MANAGE?

CHUCK TANNER TELLS a delightful story that gives us a peek behind the curtain in terms of what it's like to be a major-league manager.

"One day during the 1979 season," he says, "we were facing a left-handed pitcher and our catcher, Steve Nicosia, a right-handed hitter, was coming to the plate with the bases loaded. Somehow, I got a hunch—an unconventional hunch, certainly, but I got it. I called 'time' and waved Nicosia (who had gone four for four that day) back to the dugout. In his place I sent to the plate left-handed-hitting John Milner. Now, sending a left-handed batter against a southpaw pitcher violates one of the most fundamental of baseball strategies.

"We were playing in Pittsburgh, and the crowd of nearly 40,000 started to boo me. I said to myself, 'That's all right. They paid for their tickets. They have a right to boo if they wish.' But what really disturbed me is when I looked up into the stands and saw my own wife. She was leading the booing!

"Milner swung at the first pitch and sent the ball soaring into the right-field stands for a grand-slam home run.

"Now the crowd cheered with gusto. I was a hero."

Tanner later explained his rationale. McGraw's best pitch was a screwball. That meant a right-handed hitter was at a disadvantage, since the ball would sail away from him. If a left-handed hitter is at the plate, in reality you take away McGraw's best pitch.

Tanner, of course, had no time to make such an explanation when he sent Milner to the plate in front of the rather hostile crowd. Even if he did, only a fraction of the fans would have understood his reasoning.

"At the same time," he asks, "I wonder what the reception would be at home had Milner struck out?"

CHUCK TANNER QUOTES

MANAGING A MAJOR league baseball team has got to be one of the more frustrating jobs. The pressure of the games coupled with second-guessing fans and reporters is bound to raise the thermometer inside the most gentle of souls. Those who have been there agree that one of the best safeguards against instant insanity is the ability to maintain an optimistic outlook. The congenial manager of the '79 Bucs, Chuck Tanner, was one of the best at accentuating the positive. Some of his off-the-cuff comments reflect his enthusiasm for the game, for his team, and about life:

"I don't think a manager should be judged by whether or not he wins the pennant, but by whether he gets the most out of the 25 men he's been given."

&

"The greatest feeling in the world is to win a Major League Baseball game. The second greatest feeling is to lose a big-league game."

&

"There are three secrets to managing. The first secret is to have patience. The second is to be patient. And the third most important secret is patience."

&

"What you have to remember is that baseball isn't a week or a month, but a season—and a season is a long time."

ଛ

"You can have money piled to the ceiling, but the size of your funeral is still going to depend on the weather."

Hidden Logic

SOMETIMES THE FAN in the bleachers will voice his opinion about managerial decisions, especially when they defy logic. One of the complaints by the "experts" in the stands was why Chuck Tanner placed the Bucs' best hitter, Bill Madlock, far down in the batting order and why he had Phil Garner—a consistent long-ball hitter—batting eighth. When confronted by a reporter with these same questions, Tanner responded, "I had our best hitter for average, Bill Madlock, bat sixth and I gave him the green light to steal, which meant that Ed Ott and Phil Garner (who followed him in the line-up) would see more fastballs.

"I told Garner, who hit eighth, that he was the most important hitter on the team because he was my second cleanup hitter. I told every player to be ready, because I would use them at any time."

Hummmmmmmm. Could this be the reason why the fan remained in the stands while Mr. Tanner wore a big-league uniform?

Now that's logical.

TONY BARTIROME
Trainer

TONY BARTIROME HOLDS the dubious distinction of playing on what many fans consider the worst team in the history of the Pittsburgh Pirates—perhaps in all of baseball. The 1952 Bucs, commonly called the "Rinky Dinks" in honor of general manager Branch Rickey, the man responsible for putting the team together, lost 112 out of 154 games that year.

In this, his only major-league season, the slick-fielding first-baseman hit for a .220 average with zero home runs and only 16 RBIs. At the same time, this Pittsburgh native set a Pirate record by not hitting into one double play all year in 355 at-bats.

Military service cut short his big-league career, but he continued to play in the minors until 1963.

Tony then joined the Pirates in 1967 in another capacity—as a trainer. He was the only person in the history of Major League Baseball to make the transition from player to trainer. After 19 years in this capacity, including the championship '79 season, when manager Chuck Tanner was released by the Pirates, Bartirome moved with his friend to the Atlanta Braves as a coach in 1986.

HARVEY HADDIX
PITCHING COACH

HARVEY HADDIX WILL always be best remembered for his classic performance in Milwaukee, Wisconsin, on the night of May 26, 1959. Although he felt under the weather, he took to the mound against Lew Burdette and the heavy-hitting Braves. Haddix wasn't his usual self that night. In fact, he wasn't usual by anybody's standards. He only retired 36 consecutive batters, pitching 12 perfect innings, for one of the outstanding pitching performances of all time. Unfortunately, his Pirate teammates didn't score. In the 13th Milwaukee brought down the curtain on his moment of glory. An error, a walk and a shot over the center-field wall by slugger Joe Adcock, (who passed Hank Aaron while circling the bases) resulted in a 1-0 Braves win.

Haddix came to the Pirates from Cincinnati along with Don Hoak and Smoky Burgess in a seven-player deal. Both men were instrumental in the 1960 championship season. Haddix won Game 5 of the Series as a starter and was credited with the victory in Game 7 as a reliever when Bill Mazeroski hit what is arguably the most famous home run in baseball history.

Nicknamed "the Kitten" at St. Louis for his uncanny resemblance to Harry "the Cat" Brecheen, Haddix compiled a 136-113 record for five teams in a 14-year career. He later served as pitching coach for the Bucs during the 1979 season. He held similar positions with the Mets and Red Sox.

Harvey Haddix died in Springfield, Ohio, in 1994.

BOB SKINNER
HITTING COACH

BUCCO FANS REMEMBER the hitting coach of the '79 Pirates, Bob Skinner, for several things.

First, he enjoyed a 12-year major-league career in which he hit a lifetime .277 and clubbed 103 home runs—two of which cleared the roof at old Forbes Field. In fact, he became one of only 10 players ever to perform that feat, and the only one to do it twice. As a rookie in '54, he set a major-league record at first base with eight assists in a game. Two years later he led the National League with 54 pinch-hitting appearances. His best year was in 1958, when he hit .321 with 13 home runs and 70 RBI. Twice (1958 and 1960) he was selected to appear in the All-Star Game. He is probably best remembered by Pittsburgh fans as a starting outfielder for the legendary 1960 world champion Pirates. Three years later he was traded to Cincinnati for outfielder/pinch hitter Jerry Lynch.

Second, Skinner became manager for the Phillies. He quit after a bit less than one and a half seasons because of a lack of front-office support in his attempts to discipline controversial slugger Dick Allen. With the Phillies for parts of two seasons and with the Padres for one game, Skinner ended his managerial career with a modest 93-123 record.

Finally, he played a key role in working with hitters after he returned to the Pirates in 1979 under Chuck Tanner. He elected to move to the Braves with his manager following the '85 season.

Bob's son, Joel Skinner, became a catcher with the White Sox, Yankees and Indians. He also managed the Indians for 75 games in 2002.

HARDING "PETE" PETERSON
EXECUTIVE VICE-PRESIDENT

HARDING WILLIAM "PETE" PETERSON was a dedicated, albeit controversial, member of the staff of the '79 Bucs. Peterson loved baseball, and he genuinely loved the Pittsburgh Pirates.

Following his graduation from Rutgers, where he led the university's baseball team to the NCAA College World Series, he was signed by the Pirates. He eventually played four years as a Pirate catcher (1955-1959) and had a lifetime batting average of .273 when a broken arm resulting from a collision at home plate cut short a promising career.

Peterson refocused his talents on managing, serving nine years in the Pirates system until he was promoted to the home office as minor-league director and scouting director. In January 1979 he was appointed executive vice president, becoming responsible for the Pirates' entire baseball operation.

Peterson was best known for making bold trades—most of which turned to gold for the Bucs. His two best acquisitions were for Bill Madlock and Tim Foli, both of which appeared to be akin to armed robbery once these two stars exhibited their talents that were largely responsible for the Pirates becoming world champions during his first year as executive vice president.

As with many others in his same position, Peterson wished he could take back a few of his other deals, such as the ones that allowed pitchers John Tudor and Bert Blyleven to flee the Pirate camp with little compensation.

Whether you agreed with him or not, you could never doubt the loyalty he had toward the ball club and the dedication to his job—both of which contributed greatly in bringing the World Series trophy to the Steel City.

IF IT AIN'T BROKE. . .

"PETE" PETERSON WAS a controversial general manager for the Bucs during the '79 season. One of the ventures in which he was not a success, however, is one that even he is happy did not work.

When Peterson saw the unusual pitching motion of Kent Tekulve—the submarine pitcher who threw baseballs as though they were coming right out of the rubber slab on the mound—he was the first of many who tried to change Tekulve's delivery. He also tried to change the motion of Bruce Kison, another sidearm pitcher who was with Tekulve in the low minors at Geneva, New York, 10 years earlier. Peterson had some logical reasoning behind his counsel. He felt that, with the advent of Astroturf and the lowering of the mound beginning in 1969 from 15 inches to 10 inches, sidearm pitchers would no longer be a factor in the big leagues.

Neither of the young pitchers heeded his advice; both retained their unique style. The Pirates could not have been happier. Tekulve and Kison, as it turned out, were the only pitchers on that Geneva team to make it to the major leagues. Both also appeared in the 1979 World Series.

Tekulve still recalls this advice during his after-dinner speeches: "My standard line after telling that story in 1979 after the World Series was, 'That's how smart you have to be to be a general manager of a World Series team.'"

JOE LONNETTE
THIRD-BASE COACH

THE THIRD BASE COACH for the Bucs in 1979 was Joseph Paul Lonnett. The native of Beaver Falls, whose specialty was developing catchers, spent four years (1956-1959) behind the plate in the Phillies organization.

After compiling a mediocre .166 career batting average, Lonnett turned to managing in the minors and later joined Chuck Tanner as a coach with the White Sox and Oakland. Tanner brought him along to Pittsburgh when he came to the Pirates in that famous trade following the 1976 campaign.

ALEX MONCHAK
FIRST-BASE COACH

ALEX "AL" MONCHAK got two hits in 14 at-bats for the 1940 Philadelphia Phillies. His .143 batting average did not paint a rosy picture as a potential big-league star. In all fairness, however, his playing career was hampered by a serious injury in the minors and a long, distinguished stint in World War II, hence his nickname "Sarge."

Following a highly successful record in 13 years as a minor-league manager, he was a member of Chuck Tanner's White Sox coaching staff before being asked to join the Bucs as their first-base coach.

CHAPTER SIX

OUR ANNOUNCERS

I hear the gentle voices calling.
—Stephen Foster

BASEBALL IS A GAME of statistics and emotion. Seldom in our lives does the success or failure of an organization—one that is totally beyond our control—stir the feelings of our souls than does the baseball team with which we grew up.

Part of that loyalty was generated and enhanced by the voices we heard over radio and television.

Radio presented a different challenge to baseball broadcasters back in the '40s and '50s than did the more modern medium of television. To be a success behind the microphone in both radio and television requires an abundance of talent. The difference is that radio announcers must paint for the listeners the entire picture; television broadcasters give the viewers a frame that enhances the picture they are viewing.

In calling the play-by-play, the Pittsburgh Pirates have had a gallery of pioneers and stars over the decades. As far back as August

5, 1921, a 25-year-old Westinghouse electrical engineer and night-time studio announcer—Harold Arlin—sat in a seat behind first base at Forbes Field and described the action of a Pirates-Phillies game over KDKA radio. It was the first ever broadcast of a major league baseball game.

Since then, those who have sat in the Pirates' radio and television booths include: Rosey Rowswell, Bob Prince, Paul Long, Jim Woods, Nellie King, Milo Hamilton, Nellie Briles, Jim Rooker and the current crew of Lanny Frattare, Steve Blass, Bob Walk and Greg Brown. Because these voices come into their homes 162 times a year, Pittsburgh faithful have considered these announcers as parts of their families, albeit with a single exception.

HE NEVER HAD A CHANCE

DURING THE CHAMPIONSHIP season of 1979, Milo Hamilton was the lead voice behind the microphone. Hamilton, a veteran of 23 years in broadcasting for other teams, had earned a healthy respect among his colleagues.

Hamilton was one of America's top sports announcers, having covered major events for over a quarter of a century. Quite possibly, he participated in the play by play of more historic baseball milestones than any other broadcaster. Included in his list of memorable calls was the on-the-air description of Hank Aaron breaking Babe Ruth's all-time homer record and Roger Maris's 61st home run in 1961. In spite of his impressive resume, when this native of Fairfield, Iowa, and graduate of the University of Iowa joined the Pirates in 1976, he was in a no-win situation. The reason was simple. It was Milo Hamilton who had the unenviable task of replacing the legendary Bob Prince.

Prince had endeared himself to the hearts of Pirate fans with his unique calls of plays, his labeling of players with nicknames, his flashy clothes, his sometimes partisan description of the action and his personal stories about things that had little to do with the game he was describing. Unfortunately, some of the Pirate management were not endeared by his homespun approach and replaced him with the articulate, proper-speaking Milo Hamilton.

Hamilton's voice was clear, he used proper English, kept himself in the background and showed little emotion. In short, he was everything Bob Prince was not. And the fans did not adopt him as one of their own.

His partner at that time was a young Lanny Frattare, who understood the real story. "Milo Hamilton was going to be severely criticized no matter how solid a broadcaster he was," recalls Frattare.

Following the 1979 season, Milo Hamilton left the Bucs to become the play-by-play announcer for a second tour of duty with the Chicago Cubs from 1980-1984, before moving on to the Houston Astros where he has been since 1985.

In 1992, Milo Hamilton won the highest honor that can be given to any baseball announcer when he received the Ford C. Frick Award and was inducted into the media wing of the Baseball Hall of Fame.

GIVING THE KID A BREAK

LANNY FRATTARE, the popular voice of the Pittsburgh Pirates, was born to be an announcer. Rumor has it that he never saw a microphone he didn't like. Perhaps that love of the craft, coupled with his dedication to the Pirates, are the primary reasons Lanny has remained a familiar figure in the Bucs' broadcasting booth for a record-breaking stay since 1976.

Few know that Frattare actually got his start in major league baseball with Bob Prince. While he was describing games for the Pirates farm club in Charleston, West Virginia, Frattare visited with Prince and Nellie King in the booth. It was then that Prince unexpectedly turned to the youngster and said: "Why don't you broadcast the next half inning?" Frattare didn't flinch. He drew upon his experience as a communications graduate from Ithaca College and as a minor-league broadcaster and responded as if he were a seasoned veteran.

Later Bob Prince reportedly remarked, "I thought we'd give the kid a break and he'd enjoy the opportunity to call a big-league ball game."

That kid must have left a fine impression, because when Prince was fired, Frattare was called up to become the number-two man in the booth with Milo Hamilton.

During the onslaught of rebellion by Pirate fans against Milo Hamilton, Frattare was fortunate to dodge those bullets; Pittsburghers never considered him the one responsible for replacing their beloved Prince. The fact that Milo Hamilton was also an innocent victim in this upheaval made little difference. When Hamilton

A youthful Lanny Frattare was on his way to becoming the "Dean of Pirate Broadcasters."

left Pittsburgh after the 1979 season, Frattare was recognized and welcomed by Bucs fans as the number-one announcer.

Today Lanny supports several local charities and sponsors an annual golf tournament at St. Clair Country Club on the Monday before the All-Star Game to benefit Family Links, a nonprofit social service agency.

NOOOOOO DOUBT ABOUT IT?

HERE'S A TRIVIA QUESTION: How many times during the championship '79 season did Lanny Frattare shout out his familiar "There was noooooooooooooooo doubt about it," following a Pittsburgh win? The answer is "Zero." Lanny never used that phrase until the following year when he became the Pirates' lead announcer.

"It was a tribute to Bob Prince who used to shout at the end of a Pirate victory: 'We had 'em all the way,'" Lanny explains.

Another familiar call associated with Lanny Frattare is when he urges a long drive by a Pirate to clear the fence: "Go ball! Get outta here!"

A STRANGE BEGINNING

PIRATE ANNOUNCER GREG BROWN is a popular figure in the radio and television booths. But his start with the club did not begin behind a microphone. Instead it was inside a costume.

Brown was the back-up "Pirate Parrot" during the championship year of 1979—the inaugural year for the flamboyant mascot. At the time, Brown was an intern while attending Point Park College.

Brown later worked as the Pirates' public address announcer before serving five years as the play-by-play announcer for the Triple-A Buffalo Bisons and as a color commentator on radio broadcasts of the NFL Buffalo Bills. He joined the Bucs broadcast team in 1994.

Your Pal the "Pirate Parrot"

Could this be the start of a career in announcing for Greg Brown?

LANNY FRATTARE'S WORLD SERIES MOMENTS

IN 1979, HIS FOURTH YEAR as a Pirate announcer, Lanny Frattare had won the acclaim of Pittsburgh. Along with his partner, Milo Hamilton, Frattare was about to realize a baseball announcer's dream—to broadcast the World Series.

Pittsburgh, with its rich history and its long list of contributions to the welfare of this nation, has always been looked upon by many of the so-called image-makers of New York City as a small town that lacked "headline people." That was especially true in broadcast journalism.

Instead of inviting the local Pittsburgh announcers to describe the games, network executives elected to go with their New York-based crews. The only exposure that Frattare and Hamilton got was an occasional appearance interviewing players during a pregame or postgame show.

Chuck Finder, sports broadcasting columnist for the *Post-Gazette*, recalled how Frattare described his snub: "Even the baseball writers booted me out of the booth from which we called the play-by-play for every Pirates home game. I was only a four-year announcer at that point, so I wasn't going to open my mouth. But at least they could have let us sit in the same seats we had all year."

Frattare still has hopes of broadcasting a World Series. "I am proud of the fact I have a championship ring," he says, "but I really didn't do anything to earn it."

SEE WHAT HAPPENS WHEN YOU ASK?

ASTUTE PIRATE FANS know that Nelson Briles was one of the heroes of the 1971 World Series. This popular figure, who now makes his home in Pittsburgh, enjoyed a 14-year career with five big-league teams (including the Pirates from 1971-1973) while compiling a 129-112 mark.

After calling it quits in 1978, Briles was resigned to working at a local company and to viewing Pirate telecasts on KDKA-TV. While he felt that the announcers performed credibly, Briles thought the men in the booth could profit from someone who had "been there and done that."

Near the close of the season, he called some decision-makers at Channel 2 and suggested he be brought on board as a "color analyst"—i.e., one who could offer some insights or anecdotes for the viewing audience.

"We don't have color analysts," came the rather terse reply.

"Well, I'd make a good one," said Briles.

"Well, the bottom line is that we can't afford one," admitted the station representative.

"I'll work for free," said Briles.

Apparently, that offer was in line with the station's budget. Briles was hired for a few trial broadcasts "to see how it worked out."

Briles passed the test as would a Harvard Ph.D. in mathematics taking a seventh-grade quiz on long division. He served the entire 1979 season, and several others to follow, as a popular color man.

Today, Nellie Briles is the Pirates' vice president for corporate projects and president of the Pittsburgh Pirates Alumni Association.

CHAPTER SEVEN

NATIONAL LEAGUE CHAMPIONSHIP SERIES

Victory belongs to the most persevering.
—*Napoleon Bonaparte*

HISTORY WAS DEFINITELY NOT on the side of the Pittsburgh Pirates prior to the start of the best-of-five 1979 National League Championship Series (NLCS).

The Bucs, who certainly deserved to be in this series, had amassed a 98-64 record to capture the National League East crown by two games over the surprising Montreal Expos. Their counterparts in the National League West, the Cincinnati Reds, ended the year 90-71, edging out the second-place Houston Astros by one and a half games.

Although Pittsburgh's record was better, Cincinnati had established a well-deserved reputation as "the team to beat." Pittsburgh knew that all too well. Three times earlier in the decade—1970, 1972 and 1975—the Bucs and the Reds opposed each other in the NLCS. The Reds won each Series, sweeping the Pirates in two of the matchups. In addition, manager John McNamara and his team had defeated the Bucs eight times during their 12 encounters during the 1979 season.

Cincinnati's familiar designation as "The Big Red Machine" was no overstatement. Names of future Hall of Famers regularly appeared on the lineup cards before each game. Over the past ten years, players such as Johnny Bench and Joe Morgan had earned the respect of both the fans and the opposition with their powerful bats and sparkling defense.

The might-have-been future inductee to the Hall (one who has been since banned from baseball due to his gambling on the sport), Pete Rose, had been a vital cog in the powerful Reds organization. Rose, however, was not a factor in this dynamic '79 NLCS, for he had signed as a free agent with Philadelphia prior to the season. Likewise, two years earlier, Cincinnati lost the powerful bat of Tony Perez when he was traded to Montreal.

Along with the departure of Rose and Perez, the effects of Father Time began to show on Bench and Morgan, both of whom had lost a step or two.

These facts notwithstanding, the '79 Cincinnati club had one thing that the previous intimidating squads did not—Tom Seaver. Seaver, another future Hall of Fame inductee, was one of the game's most dominating hurlers. The former three-time Cy Young Award winner led the National League in winning percentage (.727) with a 16-6 record, including five shutouts.

Other key players for the Reds that year included infielders Ray Knight, Dave Concepcion and Dan Driessen; outfielders Dave Collins and George Foster; and pitcher Tom Hume.

Based on the team's record, savvy veterans and improved pitching, there was little wonder that bookmakers in Las Vegas cited Cincinnati as the odds-on favorite.

But that's one of the magnificent things about baseball. All these predictions mean little once the first pitch is thrown. Both the Pirates and the Reds were soon to find that to be true.

NLCS GAME 1
October 2, 1979
Riverfront Stadium • Cincinnati, Ohio

PITTSBURGH PLAYERS CHECKED into their hotel in Cincinnati on the evening of October 1, 1979, with the confidence of a team used to winning. "We felt like we were a team of destiny," said Tim Foli.

Shortstop Foli's conviction did not wane even when manager John McNamara named ace right-hander Tom Seaver as his starting pitcher for the opener of the best-of-five series at Cincinnati's Riverfront Stadium. The Bucs, in their bright gold and black uniforms, reflected a quiet confidence when they took batting practice the next day prior to the game.

Bucs manager Chuck Tanner sent to the hill John "The Candy Man" Candelaria. Tanner's selection of the 6'7" southpaw raised more than an eyebrow or two among Pittsburgh sportswriters. Although Candelaria had amassed a fine 14-9 record over the season, he had not pitched for 11 days due to a recurring back problem. The same observers noted that the once overpowering fastball, which earned for him a major league-leading earned run average (ERA) of 2.34 two years earlier, had slowed, and Candelaria had not pitched particularly well against Cincinnati that year.

If John Candelaria was overwhelmed with the statistics of those he faced that evening or discouraged by the pregame doubts raised by reporters, his performance in the first inning showed no such indication. He easily mowed down the first three batters he faced.

With no score in the game, Knight smacked a triple with one out in the bottom of the second inning, but Candelaria reached back for something extra as he struck out both Bench and Driessen to end the threat.

Phil "Scrap Iron" Garner, the eighth-place hitter, led off the Pirates' half of the third with a home run. After Candelaria struck out, Omar Moreno sent a line drive to right. Instead of allowing the ball to drop for a single, outfielder Collins attempted to make a diving catch. He missed, and the ball bounced past him to the wall. By the time the Reds got the ball back to the infield, a grinning Moreno stood on third with a triple.

Clutch hitter Tim Foli, who seemed to have a knack for finding a way to get the job done, sent a drive deep enough to the outfield to score Moreno with a sacrifice fly.

The score remained 2-0 in favor of the Pirates until the bottom of the fourth when Concepcion singled and Foster homered into the left-field stands.

Shortstop Tim Foli sensed that this was a "team of destiny."

The two pitchers kept the opposition in check for the next three innings, although Candelaria occasionally grimaced in pain as his back began to bother him.

Candelaria went to the mound in the bottom of the eighth. When manager McNamara sent up Rick Auerbach to pinch-hit for Seaver, Tanner countered with Enrique Romo, who possessed a wicked screwball. Romo retired Auerbach, but gave up a single to Collins, then walked Morgan.

With only one out and Concepcion and Foster due up, Tanner called in his ace reliever, Kent Tekulve. Tanner looked like a genius the moment Concepcion grounded into an inning-ending double play.

Cincinnati reliever Tom Hume and the Bucs' Tekulve were both up to the task of keeping the score tied through regulation play. Since Tanner had elected to pinch hit for Tekulve in the top of the tenth, he called in southpaw Grant Jackson to face the Reds in the home half of the inning. Once again Tanner appeared to be a seer; Jackson retired the side in order.

In the top of the 11th, Foli and Dave Parker led off with singles. Manager McNamara knew that slugger Willie Stargell was stepping to the plate. He could have called in one of his left-handed pitchers, such as Dave Tomlin or Fred Norman, to face the left-handed-hitting Pirate captain, but he chose to stay with the right-handed Hume.

If John McNamara had any hope of equaling Tanner's fortune in the art of decision making, it disappeared when Stargell drove Hume's first pitch high over the fence in right-center field, silencing most of the 55,006 fans. The Bucs now enjoyed a commanding 5-2 lead.

Seasoned baseball fans, however, recall the famous quote of Yogi Berra: "It ain't over 'til it's over." That insight became most apparent in the bottom half of the 11th.

Nearly half of the Reds faithful headed for the exits even before the first two Cincinnati hitters went down quietly. A few of these fans peeked over their shoulders to watch, however, as the next two batters reached base with a single and a walk. Some of them stopped, made an about-face, scurried back to their seats and joined in the cheers as reliable slugger Johnny Bench stepped into the batter's box.

Bench, who had already become a legend in the Queen City, had the stage set for another heroic act. Tanner signaled to the bullpen for right-hander Don Robinson to replace Jackson. Robinson, normally a starting pitcher, had a wicked curve ball that broke down and away from a right-handed hitter. With a 3-2 count on Bench, Robinson tried to get the Cincinnati catcher to chase a low, outside curve ball. The savvy Bench didn't offer at the pitch that was called a ball by home-plate umpire John Kibler.

The bases were loaded. Two men were out. Cincinnati, with one long belt over the fence could now win the game. The volume of cheering rose as up to the plate stepped Ray Knight, a .318 hitter who had smacked 10 home runs that year.

This was the sort of situation that makes baseball the greatest sport in the universe.

Reds fans continued to scream in support of the batter who had quickly dug himself into a hole by taking two quick strikes. The next pitch was low for a ball.

Robinson used the same strategy on Knight as he did with Bench. He broke off a sharp curve that landed in the dirt outside the strike zone. Knight, however, fell for the ploy. He swung and missed.

That should have ended the game had the ball not skipped two feet behind catcher Ed Ott. Ott quickly retrieved it and, instead of stepping on home plate to register a game-ending force out, stopped the hearts of the Pittsburgh fans watching the game on television when he instinctively threw the ball to first. Stargell, however, remained alert, caught the ball and calmly stepped on the bag, retiring Knight and the Reds.

The final score was Pittsburgh 5, Cincinnati 2, in a game that will long be remembered by fans of both teams.

Game 1
Time: 3:14 • Attendance: 55,006

	1	2	3	4	5	6	7	8	9	10	11	R
Pirates	0	0	2	0	0	0	0	0	0	0	3	5
Reds	0	0	0	2	0	0	0	0	0	0	0	2

Pittsburgh	ab	r	h	bi	Cincinnati	ab	r	h	bi
Moreno, cf	5	1	1	0	Collins, rf	5	0	2	0
Foli, ss	4	0	2	1	Morgan, 2b	4	0	0	0
Alexander, pr	0	1	0	0	Concepcion, ss	5	1	2	0
B.Robinson, lf	0	0	0	0	Foster, lf	3	1	1	2
Parker, rf	4	1	1	0	Bench, c	3	0	2	0
Stargell, 1b	4	1	1	3	Knight, 3b	5	0	0	0
Milner, lf	5	0	0	0	Driessen, 1b	4	0	0	0
Stennett, 2b	0	0	0	0	Cruz, cf	4	0	0	0
Madlock, 3b	5	0	2	0	Seaver, p	2	0	0	0
Ott, c	5	0	1	0	Auerbach, ph	1	0	0	0
Garner, 2b	4	1	2	1	Hume, p	1	0	0	0
Candelaria, p	3	0	0	0	Tomlin, p	0	0	0	0
Romo, p	0	0	0	0					
Tekulve, p	0	0	0	0					
Easler, ph	1	0	0	0					
Jackson, p	1	0	0	0					
D.Robinson, p	0	0	0	0					
Totals	**41**	**5**	**10**	**5**		**37**	**2**	**7**	**2**

DP: Pirates 2, Reds 1; 3B: Bench, Moreno; HR: Garner, Foster, Stargell; SB: Madlock (2), Collins

Pittsburgh Pitching	IP	H	R	ER	BB	SO
Candelaria	7	2	2	2	1	4
Romo	1/3	1	0	0	1	0
Tekulve	1 2/3	0	0	0	1	0
Jackson (W)	1 2/3	1	0	0	1	2
D Robinson (S)	1/3	0	0	0	1	1
Cincinnati Pitching						
Seaver	8	5	2	2	2	5
Hume (L)	2 1/3	5	3	3	0	1
Tomlin	2/3	0	0	0	1	1

NLCS GAME 2
October 3, 1979
Riverfront Stadium • Cincinnati, Ohio

GAME 2 OF THE NLCS featured three unusual losses: Kent Tekulve lost a strike, Willie Stargell lost a base runner and a veteran umpire lost a ball.

A jam-packed crowd of 55,000 fans at Riverfront Stadium knew that it was a crucial game. Were their Reds to lose this contest, they would have to face the Pirates on their home turf on the short end of a 0-2 record in this best-of-five-game playoff.

Hoping to stop the momentum of the previous evening's extra-inning victory by the Bucs, manager John McNamara sent right-handed pitcher Frank Pastore to the hill. Pastore was a questionable choice. Not only had he posted a modest 6-7 record and 4.25 ERA during the regular season, Pastore was also a rookie. He was thus dropped into a pressure-cooker situation that would normally be reserved for more seasoned players.

Starting for the Bucs was Jim Bibby, a more logical choice. This eight-year veteran right-hander entered the game with a 12-4 record and an impressive 2.81 ERA.

After the game got underway, Pastore did not appear unnerved by the situation. In fact, it was his sacrifice fly in the second inning that gave Cincinnati a 1-0 lead.

The Bucs tied it in their half of the fourth when Bill Madlock grounded into a force play, scoring Tim Foli from third. But they could have, and should have, gotten more than one run.

Foli led off the inning with a single. Dave "the Cobra" Parker followed with another, sending Foli to second. To the plate strode big Willie Stargell. The veteran slugger lofted a fly to deep left. Cincinnati left-fielder George Foster drifted back a few steps and appeared ready to catch the ball. Foli wisely tagged at second, and Parker remained halfway between first and second.

Foster misjudged the ball that sailed over his head and hit the base of the outfield wall. It bounced straight back into Foster's glove, allowing Foli to get to third, but no farther. Parker easily made it to second.

Stargell, meanwhile, failed to watch the base runner ahead of him and was tooling into second before he saw Parker occupying the bag. Stargell quickly made a U-turn as fast as his 6'2 1/2", 225-pound body would allow. Even a headlong dive into first base was not enough to avoid the relay toss from Dave Concepcion to Dan Driessen. Willie was out, thus erasing the potential for a big rally.

With the score knotted at one, Pirate leadoff hitter "Scrap Iron" Garner smacked a crisp, sinking liner to right-center field to begin the fifth inning. Cincinnati right-fielder Dave Collins dashed toward the ball, dove and reached out with his glove as far as his 5'11" body would allow and grabbed the ball. Collins lost his balance; he slipped, slid and tumbled on the surface before leaping to his feet and showing everyone the ball held tightly in his glove.

It was a sensational catch to everyone who saw it . . . well, almost everyone. Second-base umpire Frank Pulli flashed the "safe" sign, indicating that Collins had trapped the ball.

With Garner standing on first, manager McNamara called time and ran toward Pulli, screaming in protest. Collins charged in from right field singing the same song. Tempers flared. Words became stronger. "Ask him! Ask him!" demanded Collins, pointing toward right-field umpire John Kibler. Kibler also gave the "safe" sign, although he later confessed to not seeing the play.

Joe Morgan of the Reds became mediator and peacemaker as he pulled the irate Collins away from Umpire Pulli.

Pulli, as expected, did not change his call, and Collins maintained that he had caught the ball.

After the dust settled and emotions cooled, Foli lined a double past Ray Knight down the third-base line that scored Garner, giving the Bucs a 2-1 lead.

The score remained the same in the home half of the eighth when Chuck Tanner called in a parade of relief pitchers. After Grant Jackson retired the first batter, Enrique Romo gave up two singles. Enter Kent Tekulve who wild-pitched the runners to second and third, struck out Johnny Bench, intentionally walked Driessen and got Ray Knight to send a lazy fly ball into the glove of center-fielder Moreno.

Tekulve struck out the first batter in the bottom of the ninth. On a 1-1 count, pinch hitter Hector Cruz swung and missed the next pitch. Unbeknownst to Tekulve, umpires Jim Quick and Dick Stello had called time because of a loose ball from the bullpen. Thus, the strike did not count. The call may have unnerved the Bucs pitcher as Cruz promptly knocked a double between Moreno and Parker, and Collins followed with another two-bagger to tie the score.

Dave Roberts replaced Tekulve and promptly walked Morgan on four pitches. As the Cincinnati faithful cheered in anticipation of a winning rally, Tanner brought in Don Robinson, the man who struck out Bench with the bases full the night before to preserve the win. Robinson again donned the mantle of "super-stopper" as he got Concepcion on strikes and Foster on a routine grounder to second to send the game to extra innings.

Former Bucs farmhand Doug Bair worked the tenth inning for Cincinnati. Omar Moreno singled up the middle, Foli laid down one of his familiar near-perfect sacrifice bunts and Parker laced a single to right, scoring Moreno with the go-ahead run.

Robinson set the Reds down one-two-three. The Bucs celebrated a hard-earned 3-2 win and took a commanding two-games-to-none lead.

At an impromptu press conference following the victory, Stargell could make light of his base-running goof: "Chuck [Tanner] has taught us a lot of things, but he never taught any of us how to run from second to first base. Imagine, two, no three Buccos on second base. Then an old beer truck like me slides headfirst into the bag."

Meanwhile, in the Cincinnati clubhouse, Dave Collins stood in front of his locker and repeated in a voice now hoarse from an hour of shouting to any reporter willing to listen: "I caught the ball! I caught the ball!"

NBC television announcer and former Yankee shortstop Tony Kubek viewed instant replays of the catch. "I watched the replay many times," he said, "and every time Collins caught the ball."

When Kubek brought up the results of the replays to Umpire Pulli, the veteran umpire gritted his teeth and snapped: "%#@*@ the replay! Don't tell me about %^$*@* replays!"

Game 2
Time: 3:24 • Attendance: 55,000

	1	2	3	4	5	6	7	8	9	10	R
Pirates	0	0	0	1	1	0	0	0	0	1	3
Reds	0	1	0	0	0	0	0	0	1	0	2

	Pittsburgh					*Cincinnati*			
	ab	r	h	bi		ab	r	h	bi
Moreno, cf	5	1	2	0	Collins, rf	5	0	1	1
Foli, ss	4	1	2	1	Morgan, 2b	3	0	0	0
Parker, rf	5	0	2	1	Concepcion, ss	5	0	2	0
Stargell, 1b	3	0	2	0	Foster, lf	3	0	1	0
Milner, lf	2	0	0	0	Bench, c	5	0	0	0
B.Robinson, lf	2	0	0	0	Driessen, 1b	4	1	1	0
Madlock, 3b	5	0	0	1	Knight, 3b	5	0	2	0
Ott, c	4	0	2	0	Geronimo, cf	3	0	0	0
Garner, 2b	4	1	1	0	Pastore, p	0	0	0	1
Bibby, p	0	0	0	0	Spilman, ph	1	0	0	0
Jackson, p	0	0	0	0	Tomlin, p	0	0	0	0
Romo, p	0	0	0	0	Hume, p	0	0	0	0
Tekulve, p	1	0	0	0	Cruz, ph	1	1	1	0
Roberts, p	0	0	0	0	Bair, p	0	0	0	0
D.Robinson, p	0	0	0	0					
Totals	35	3	11	3		35	2	8	2

DP: Reds 1; 2B: Concepcion, Foli, Stargell, Cruz, Collins;
SB: Morgan, Knight, Collins

Pittsburgh Pitching	IP	H	R	ER	BB	SO
Bibby	7	4	1	1	4	5
Jackson	1/3	0	0	0	0	
Romo	0	2	0	0	0	0
Tekulve	1	2	1	1	1	2
Roberts	0	0	0	0	1	0
D Robinson (W)	1 2/3	0	0	0	0	2
Cincinnati Pitching						
Pastore	7	7	2	2	3	1
Tomlin	2/3	1	0	0	0	1
Bair (L)	2/3	2	1	1	1	0

NLCS GAME 3
October 5, 1979
Three Rivers Stadium • Pittsburgh, Pennsylvania

EARLIER IN THE SEASON, Bucs pitcher Bert Blyleven was eager to leave the team because his manager would not allow him to finish some games, even though he was pitching well and felt strong. He publicly accused his field general of being too quick with "the hook." In spite of the criticism leveled against him, manager Chuck Tanner selected this same pitcher to start Game 3 of the NLCS in Pittsburgh.

The Bucs got off to a positive start when, in the bottom of the first, Omar Moreno walked to open the inning. Moreno, with 77 stolen bases during the regular season, had not swiped a base in the playoffs . . . until now. He clearly beat the throw from Cincinnati catcher Johnny Bench and stood on second with nobody out. He took off for third when Tim Foli hit a high chopper to short. Dave Concepcion threw high to Ray Knight covering third, and Moreno slid headfirst to beat the toss. He scored on a sacrifice fly off the bat of Dave Parker.

In inning number two, with the Bucs still leading, 1-0, Phil Garner opened with a hit to right. When the ball skipped past out-fielder Dave Collins, Garner wound up on third with a triple. Foli's sacrifice fly scored Garner with the second Pirate run.

After a third scoreless inning by the Reds, the Bucs came out swinging. Willie Stargell slammed one into the right-field stands, earning for himself a "curtain call" from vocal Pittsburgh fans. One out later, Bill Madlock homered and was given the same encore treatment by the fans, who became more enthusiastic as the game progressed.

The next inning gave them additional encouragement. Blyleven helped his own cause with a single. After Moreno sacrificed him to second, Parker walked with two out. As if to say, "It's all over but the shouting," Willie Stargell sent a rope over first base for a double, scoring both runners.

Blyleven lost his shutout in the visitors' half of the sixth when Bench lined a 3-2 pitch high over the left-field wall.

"I wanted to finish this one," recalled Blyleven. "When Bench hit the homer, it upset me. I had to make sure that I concentrated on the next batter. I had to force myself because I wanted to finish."

With the Pirates leading, 6-1, at the start of the seventh inning, a dozen of the players' wives, led by Pam Nicosia, wife of catcher Steve Nicosia, plus about 40 other women, jumped on the platform behind home plate and atop the Pirates' dugout. They danced and sang the refrain of the Bucs' theme song "We Are Fam-a-Lee!" Most of the 42,240 fans joined in. It may have not been the Mormon Tabernacle Choir, but the music was certainly heavenly to any Pittsburgh fan.

Steve Nicosia might not have contributed directly to the Pirates sweep in the NLCS, but his wife, Pam, sure did. She led the players' wives in a rendition of "We Are Fam-a-Lee" from atop the Pirates' dugout.

The song may have spurred on Bert Blyleven, who looked like Cy Young as he retired the last nine batters. In the meantime, the Bucs added one more run in the bottom half of the eighth, aided by center fielder Cesar Geronimo's error.

When Geronimo took a sharp breaking curve ball for a called strike three to end the Reds' ninth inning, the final score read Pittsburgh 7, Cincinnati 1. The Bucs were now champions of the National League. The team and the world's greatest fans prepared to take on the American League Champion Baltimore Orioles in the 1979 World Series.

Heroes of the final NLCS game were Willie Stargell, who was given the trophy as MVP, and pitcher Bert Blyleven, who tossed a complete game, walked none, struck out nine and scattered just eight hits.

Blyleven never got in serious trouble throughout the entire nine innings. As *Post-Gazette* assistant sports editor, Marino Parascenzo, observed, "His fast ball was zippy, and his curve ball was bending like a five-cent cigar."

Perhaps the best commentary on Blyleven's superb performance was the fact that manager Tanner, who had worn a path from the dugout to the mound that year, never once left the bench for a discussion with his pitcher. As to why he did not visit the mound while Blyleven was pitching, Tanner put it pointedly: "Bert told me to stay in the dugout."

Game 3
Time: 2:45 • Attendance: 42,240

	1	2	3	4	5	6	7	8	9	R
Reds	0	0	0	0	0	1	0	0	0	1
Pirates	1	1	2	2	0	0	0	1	x	7

Cincinnati	ab	r	h	bi	Pittsburgh	ab	r	h	bi
Collins, rf	4	0	2	0	Moreno, cf	2	1	0	0
Morgan, 2b	4	0	0	0	Foli, ss	4	0	0	1
Concepcion, ss	4	0	2	0	Parker, rf	3	1	1	1
Foster, lf	4	0	0	0	Stargell, 1b	4	1	2	3
Bench, c	4	1	1	1	Milner, lf	2	0	0	0
Driessen, 1b	4	0	0	0	B.Robinson, lf	1	0	0	0
Knight, 3b	4	0	2	0	Madlock, 3b	2	1	1	1
Geronimo, cf	4	0	1	0	Ott, c	4	0	0	0
LaCoss, p	0	0	0	0	Garner, 2b	4	2	2	0
Norman, p	1	0	0	0	Blyleven, p	3	1	1	0
Leibrandt, p	0	0	0	0					
Soto, p	0	0	0	0					
Spilman, ph	1	0	0	0					
Auerbach, ph	1	0	0	0					
Tomlin, p	0	0	0	0					
Hume, p	0	0	0	0					
Totals	**35**	**1**	**8**	**1**		**29**	**7**	**7**	**6**

E: Geronimo; 2B: Knight, Stargell; 3B: Garner; HR: Stargell, Madlock, Bench; SB: Moreno, Parker

Cincinnati Pitching	IP	H	R	ER	BB	SO
LaCoss (L)	1 2/3	1	2	2	4	0
Norman	2	4	4	4	1	1
Leibrandt	1/3	0	0	0	0	0
Soto	2	0	0	0	0	1
Tomlin	1 2/3	2	1	0	1	1
Hume	1/3	0	0	0	0	0
Pittsburgh Pitching						
Blyleven (W)	9	8	1	1	0	9

Pirates NLCS Statistics

Player:	Avg.	AB	R	H	2B	3B	HR	RBI	SB
Matt Alexander, pr	.000	0	1	0	0	0	0	0	0
Jim Bibby, p	.000	0	0	0	0	0	0	0	0
Bert Blyleven, p	.333	3	1	1	0	0	0	0	0
John Candelaria, p	.000	3	0	0	0	0	0	0	0
Mike Easler, ph	.000	1	0	0	0	0	0	0	0
Tim Foli, ss	.333	12	1	4	1	0	0	3	0
Phil Garner, 2b	.417	12	4	5	0	1	1	1	0
Grant Jackson, p	.000	1	0	0	0	0	0	0	0
Bill Madlock, 3b	.250	12	1	3	0	0	1	2	2
John Milner, of	.000	9	0	0	0	0	0	0	0
Omar Moreno, of	.250	12	3	3	0	1	0	0	1
Ed Ott, c	.231	13	0	3	0	0	0	0	0
Dave Parker, of	.333	12	2	4	0	0	0	2	1
Dave Roberts, p	.000	0	0	0	0	0	0	0	0
Don Robinson, p	.000	0	0	0	0	0	0	0	0
Bill Robinson, of	.000	3	0	0	0	0	0	0	0
Enrique Romo, p	.000	0	0	0	0	0	0	0	0
Willie Stargell, 1b	.455	11	2	5	2	0	2	6	0
Rennie Stennett, 2b	.000	0	0	0	0	0	0	0	0
Kent Tekulve, p	.000	1	0	0	0	0	0	0	0
Total	**.267**	**105**	**15**	**28**	**3**	**2**	**4**	**14**	**4**

Pitcher:	W	L	ERA	G	IP	H	ER	BB	SO
Jim Bibby	0	0	1.29	1	7.0	4	1	4	5
Bert Blyleven	1	0	1.00	1	9.0	8	1	0	9
John Candelaria	0	0	2.57	1	7.0	5	2	1	4
Grant Jackson	1	0	0.00	2	2.0	1	0	1	2
Dave Roberts	0	0	0.00	1	0.0	0	0	1	0
Don Robinson	1	0	0.00	2	2.0	0	0	1	3
Enrique Romo	0	0	0.00	2	0.1	3	0	1	1
Kent Tekulve	0	0	3.38	2	2.2	2	1	2	2
Total	**3**	**0**	**1.50**		**30.0**	**23**	**5**	**11**	**26**

CHAPTER EIGHT

THE WORLD SERIES

And he shall have dominion over the birds.

—Genesis 1:28

BOB PRINCE WOULD HAVE EXCLAIMED, "We had 'em all the way!"

Following the 1979 World Series, *Sports Illustrated* astutely observed: "In truth, the Pirates won the world championship more than the Orioles lost it."

After being behind the mighty Orioles three games to one, other teams may have folded. Not the Pirates. Instead, they marched to the beat not of a different drum, but of a different tune. "We Are Fam-a-Lee" became a battle cry that caused players to dig deep inside for strength and confidence. By beating Baltimore's best pitchers and holding its hitters to only two runs in the final three games, Pittsburgh became a team of destiny. It's as if the gods of baseball pronounced the Pirates as world champions even before the first pitch of the opening game on October 10, 1979.

Let your mind return to that never-to-be-forgotten fall classic. Because you know the ending, as you read these accounts, you can repeat with the utmost confidence, "We had 'em all the way!"

WORLD SERIES GAME 1
October 10, 1979
Memorial Stadium • Baltimore, Maryland

THE TEMPERATURE DIPPED well below the 40-degree mark on October 10, 1979, as the American League Champion Baltimore Orioles prepared to play host to the champions of the National League, the Pittsburgh Pirates. The nippy weather was not surprising, since the scheduled opener the evening before was snowed out. During the hours before the game, helicopters hovered over the outfield grass and kerosene was poured onto the ground and set afire in an attempt to dry out the field. "I think it was the coldest World Series game in history," recalls Pirate outfielder Bill Robinson.

Before the start of the game, a local character named "Wild Bill" Hagy did his best to ignite the flames of passion inside the 53,735 Bird watchers through a bizarre pregame ritual. Using gestures akin to the singing group known as The Village People, who spelled out letters to the popular song "YMCA," this pudgy Baltimore taxi driver, dressed in his familiar orange T-shirt, blue jeans and white cowboy hat, stood atop the home team dugout and shaped his arms and body to spell-out: "O-R-I-O-L-E-S." Bird fans shouted out the letters in concert with a volume akin to the tenth power squared.

Baltimore fielded a team deserving of respect. They got to the Series by finishing the regular season eight games in front of the Milwaukee Brewers and 13 1/2 games ahead of the World champion New York Yankees. They proceeded to best the California Angels in four games to win the American League pennant. Led by their scrappy manager, Earl Weaver, the Birds fielded a combination of veterans and youngsters who did whatever they could to win games.

The talents of regulars Doug DeCinces, Rick Dempsey, Al Bumbry, Mark Belanger, Ken Singleton, Kiko Garcia and Eddie Murray were enhanced by a supporting cast of Benny Ayala, John Lowenstein, Pat Kelly and Terry Crowley. The pitching staff was headed by soon-to-be-named Cy Young Award Winner for that year, Mike Flanagan, who led the majors with 23 wins. Tippy Martinez, Dennis Martinez, Scott McGregor and future Hall of Famer Jim Palmer also pitched with distinction.

Following an opening-night rainout, the lean and limber Pirates were eager to show the Orioles and the rest of the baseball world that they also belonged in the fall classic. Bruce Kison (13-7 for the season and a rookie in the '71 Series) took the hill for manager Chuck Tanner's crew. His mound opponent was the Orioles' ace, southpaw Mike Flanagan.

In the home half of the first, things did not look good for the Bucs. Baltimore's leadoff hitter, Al Bumbry, hit a soft liner to left for a single. Two of the next three batters reached base on walks. With the bases loaded and only one out, the Pirates appeared destined to get out of the inning without further damage when Lowenstein hit what looked like a sure double-play grounder to second base, but Scrap Iron Garner "double clutched" as he attempted to get a grip on the wet ball. When he threw to Tim Foli covering second, the ball looked like a bar of soap as it slipped out of his hands and sailed over Foli's head into center field. The Orioles scored two runs. A wild pitch led to another tally.

With Baltimore in front 3-0, Pirate captain Willie Stargell strolled to the mound to calm Kison and to convince him that he could retire the remaining hitters. The next batter, Doug DeCinces, obviously didn't believe him. He sent a Kison pitch high into the night and deep into the stands for two more runs.

Those five runs by the Orioles set a Series record for an opening inning of Game 1.

Perhaps of equal importance was the fact that due to the cold, wet weather, Kison lost feeling in his pitching hand and was unavailable for the remainder of the Series.

Pirate pitchers Jim Rooker, Enrique Romo and Don Robinson collectively shut out the O's over the next four innings.

As the temperature dropped even more, and steam came from the mouths of the players, Foli singled in the Pirates' fourth and cruised into third on Dave Parker's single. He eventually scored on Stargell's infield out.

In the top of the sixth, Flanagan appeared to be breezing by with a comfortable 5-1 lead. Pirate bats abruptly came alive when singles by Parker and Bill Robinson, coupled with a DeCinces error on a grounder by catcher Steve Nicosia, loaded the bases. With two outs, Phil Garner singled home two runs.

In the eighth, "Pops" smacked a Flanagan fastball into the right-field stands, narrowing the gap to 5-4. "Flanagan has two curve balls," said Stargell. "One is a good, hard curve ball. The other one you can run into the clubhouse, get a drink of water and still get back in time to hit." It was one of those slow curve balls that he hit out.

The score remained that way until the Pirates' half of the ninth when, with two outs and Parker standing on third base with the potential tying run, Captain Stargell showed everyone he was but a mere human; he lifted a weak pop-up to shortstop Mark Belanger for the final out of the game.

Garner and Stargell collected two RBIs during the game, and Dave "the Cobra" Parker finished with four hits. These impressive statistics mattered little to Bucs fans, as Baltimore now led the Series one game to none. Nevertheless, everyone in Pittsburgh was convinced that the Fam-a-Lee remained alive.

"After the game," said Parker, "for the first time all year I saw a hint of defeat in the eyes of the team. I gathered all the players around me and reminded them that even though we were down by five runs in the first inning, we almost pulled this one out. I told them that we could beat these guys. I told them that we were the ones, the only ones who deserved to be world champions."

Following Parker's mini pep rally, the players started to celebrate as if they had just won the first game of opening day. They grabbed for some crab legs that had been sent to the clubhouse and popped a few cans of beer. This was the sort of unbridled confidence that could be had by 25 men who truly believed in themselves.

Game 1
Time: 3:18 • Attendance: 53,735

	1	2	3	4	5	6	7	8	9	R
Pirates	0	0	0	1	0	2	0	1	0	4
Orioles	5	0	0	0	0	0	0	0	x	5

Pittsburgh	ab	r	h	bi	Baltimore	ab	r	h	bi
Moreno, cf	5	0	0	0	Bumbry, cf	4	1	1	0
Foli, ss	5	1	1	0	Belanger, ss	3	1	0	0
Parker, rf	5	1	4	0	Singleton, rf	3	0	1	0
B.Robinson, lf	5	1	1	0	Murray, 1b	2	1	1	0
Stargell, 1b	5	1	1	2	Lowenstein, lf	4	1	0	1
Madlock, 3b	3	0	0	0	Roenick, lf	0	0	0	0
Nicosia, c	4	0	0	0	DeCinces, 3b	3	1	1	2
Garner, 2b	4	0	3	2	Smith, 2b	2	0	1	0
Kison, p	0	0	0	0	Dauer, 2b	1	0	1	0
Rooker, p	1	0	0	0	Dempsey, c	4	0	0	0
Sanguillen, ph	1	0	0	0	Flanagan, p	4	0	0	0
Romo, p	0	0	0	0					
D.Robinson, p	0	0	0	0					
Jackson, p	0	0	0	0					
Lacy, ph	1	0	0	0					
Stennett, ph	1	0	1	0					
Totals	**40**	**4**	**11**	**4**		**30**	**5**	**6**	**3**

Errors: Garner, Foli, Stargell, DeCinces 2, Belanger; DP: Pirates 1; 2B: Parker, Garner; HR: DeCinces, Stargell; SB: Murray

Pittsburgh Pitching	IP	H	R	ER	BB	SO
Kison (L)	1/3	3	5	4	2	0
Rooker	3 2/3	2	0	0	1	2
Romo	1	0	0	0	2	0
D. Robinson	2	0	0	0	1	1
Jackson	1	1	0	0	0	1
Baltimore Pitching						
Flanagan (W)	9	11	4	2	1	7

WORLD SERIES GAME 2
October 11, 1979
Memorial Stadium • Baltimore, Maryland

GAMBLING ON GAMES by players and managers is strictly prohibited in baseball. At the same time, field managers often must toss the dice when it comes to strategy, depending on the circumstances. Nobody knew this better than the Pirates' Chuck Tanner and the Orioles' Earl Weaver.

Game 2 of the '79 World Series would show that sometimes the dice can be your friend; at other times your enemy.

Miserable weather in Baltimore continued to plague the Series. A rainy night left the grass at Memorial Stadium slippery, providing a hazard for outfielders.

Singles by Willie Stargell, John Milner and Bill Madlock, plus a sacrifice fly off the bat of Ed Ott in Pittsburgh's half of the second inning, staked the Bucs to a two-run lead off of Baltimore's legendary pitcher, Jim Palmer. Yet even the most optimistic Bucs fan knew those runs would not hold up. That conviction was justified when, in the bottom half of the inning, with Baltimore fans chanting: "Ed-dee . . . Ed-dee . . . Ed-dee. . . ," slugger Eddie Murray propelled Pirate starter Bert Blyleven's changeup into the right-field stands, narrowing the Pirates' lead to one run.

Following this spurt of offense, both Palmer and Blyleven held opponents' bats relatively quiet, until, with Ken Singleton on first, Murray again brought the partisan Baltimore crowd to life with a game-tying double in the home half of the sixth.

Don Robinson replaced Blyleven in the seventh inning and kept the Birds scoreless for two frames.

Baltimore twice came close to pulling ahead. The first such occasion happened earlier in the game when Pirate right fielder Dave Parker uncorked a terrific throw on one hop to catcher Ed Ott to cut down Eddie Murray who was attempting to come home on a sacrifice fly. The next time was in the eighth inning. Baltimore had two men on with no outs. It was a perfect situation for a sacrifice bunt. But manager Earl Weaver, who should never be confused with someone who always did the expected, opted to have John

Lownstein swing away. This time one of his daring ploys failed to work, and Lowenstein grounded into a double play.

Later Weaver was philosophical about his strategy: "When you shoot craps, sometimes you lose."

In the top half of the ninth, with Tippy Martinez starting his second inning of relief, pinch hitter Bill Robinson singled. Don Stanhouse relieved Martinez, and Matt Alexander ran for Robinson. The speedy Alexander attempted to advance into scoring position with a steal of second. He was cut down by a perfect throw by catch-

World Series heroes sometimes come in the most unlikely of persons, like reserve catcher Manny Sanguillen.

er Rick Dempsey. This was one gamble that failed to pay off for manager Tanner. Following a second out, Ed Ott singled off the chest of second baseman Billy Smith. Phil Garner moved Ott to second with a walk. With two men on and two outs, pinch hitter Manny Sanguillen, who had had only four RBI during the entire season, gave the Bucs a lift when this notorious "bad ball hitter" blistered an outside pitch on a line to right. Ott lumbered around third with all the grace of a catcher. Ken Singleton picked up the ball from the wet turf and fired it toward home. Instead of allowing the ball to go through, first baseman Murray elected to cut off the throw and relay it to catcher Dempsey. Racing the relay throw to the plate, Ott executed a fade-away slide that would have been the envy of Ty Cobb, barely avoiding Dempsey's attempted tag.

Many observers felt that Murray should have let the ball go through. But even Chuck Tanner felt it was a proper choice. "The field was soggy," he said. "You never know what the ball would have done. It might have stuck. It was an intelligent play by Murray."

With Pittsburgh leading 3-2, Kent Tekulve went to the mound with the challenge to once again perform his magic as a closer. As described by veteran sportscaster Vin Scully, Tekulve "wheeled like a unicycle on a seesaw" when he struck out the first two hitters. The last Oriole recorded the final out of the inning, and the game, with a routine pop fly out to the infield.

That play closed the book on Game 2. The dice simply rolled in favor of the Pirates. The Series was tied at one game apiece, and the action moved on to the Steel City.

World Series Game 3
October 12, 1979
Three Rivers Stadium • Pittsburgh, Pennsylvania

Tossing out the first pitch of Game 3 of the 1979 World Series on October 12 in Pittsburgh was Katie Murtaugh, widow of former Pirate skipper Danny Murtaugh, who led the Bucs to their previous two world championships in 1960 and 1971. Pirate fans and players hoped that some of that winning spirit would be contagious.

Game 2
Time: 3:13 • Attendance: 53,739

	1	2	3	4	5	6	7	8	9	R
Pirates	0	2	0	0	0	0	0	0	1	3
Orioles	0	1	0	0	0	1	0	0	0	2

Pittsburgh	ab	r	h	bi	Baltimore	ab	r	h	bi
Moreno, cf	5	0	1	0	Bumbry, cf	5	0	0	0
Foli, ss	4	0	1	0	Belanger, ss	3	0	0	0
Parker, rf	4	0	1	0	Crowley, ph	0	0	0	0
Stargell, 1b	4	1	1	0	T. Martinez, p	0	0	0	0
Milner, lf	3	1	1	0	Stanhouse, p	0	0	0	0
B.Robinson, ph	1	0	1	0	Singleton, rf	4	1	1	0
Alexander, lf	0	0	0	0	Murray, 1b	3	1	3	2
Madlock, 3b	4	0	2	1	DeCinces, 3b	4	0	0	0
Ott, c	3	1	1	1	Lowenstein, lf	3	0	1	0
Garner, 2b	2	0	1	0	Smith, 2b	4	0	0	0
Blyleven, p	2	0	0	0	Dempsey, c	3	0	1	0
Easler, ph	0	0	0	0	Palmer, p	2	0	0	0
D. Robinson, p	0	0	0	0	Kelly, ph	0	0	0	0
Sanguillen, ph	1	0	1	1	Garcia, ss	1	0	0	0
Tekulve, p	0	0	0	0					
Totals	**33**	**3**	**11**	**3**		**32**	**2**	**6**	**2**

Errors: Parker, DeCinces, Foli; DP: Pirates 3, Orioles 2; 2B: Murray; HR: Murray

Pittsburgh Pitching	IP	H	R	ER	BB	SO
Blyleven	6	5	2	2	2	0
D. Robinson (W)	2	1	0	0	3	2
Tekulve (S)	1	0	0	0	0	2
Baltimore Pitching						
Palmer	7	8	2	2	2	3
T. Martinez	1	1	0	0	0	1
Stanhouse (L)	1	2	1	1	1	0

Adding to the enthusiasm and rhythmic clapping of the more than 50,000 partisan Pirate fans, blaring from the speakers surrounding Three Rivers Stadium was the theme song of the '79 Bucs—"We Are Fam-a-Lee!"

Even the lettering atop the Pirates' dugout spelled out that label.

John "Candy Man" Candelaria (14-9 during the regular season) was manager Tanner's choice to start the pivotal game against the Orioles' Scott McGregor who earned a respectable 13-6 record over the season and a league-leading "opponents' on-base percentage" of .275.

In the first two innings, Pirate hitters looked as though they would make a mockery of that statistic. Omar Moreno doubled in the first, moved to third on McGregor's balk and scored on a sacrifice fly by Dave Parker. In the second, Willie Stargell singled. Steve Nicosia sent him to second with another single. Both runners scored on a double by Phil Garner.

Behind 3-0, Baltimore began to peck away in the third. Following a walk to Kiko Garcia, Benny Ayala—a surprise starter who had hit only six home runs all year—showed some hidden power when he smacked a two-run round-tripper and brought the Birds to within one run.

Following a 67-minute rain delay, the Candy Man seemed to have problems with his footing on the slippery surface of the mound. He also had a few problems with batters such as Rich Dauer, who led off the fourth with a double to left. Dempsey followed with another double to right, although Dauer was able to get only to third. Normally "automatic" Tim Foli's error loaded the bases. Garcia got another of his four hits that day (two singles, a double and a triple) when he knocked in three of his four runs with a ringing three-base-hit to right. What followed was an even more potent Oriole offense plus an anemic Pirate defense. Enrique Romo relieved a weary Candelaria and promptly hit pinch hitter Al Bumbry. Ken Singleton's single scored Garcia and moved Bumbry to third. Doug DeCinces hit a fielder's choice to second, but Garner's wild throw to first allowed Bumbry to score. The unlikely power combination of Garcia and Ayala paced the Orioles to a 7-3 lead.

The Bucs got a run in the sixth when Madlock singled home Stargell, who had doubled. Baltimore countered when Dempsey doubled, and Garcia got him home with a single.

Game 3
Time: 2:51 • Attendance: 50,848

	1	2	3	4	5	6	7	8	9	R
Orioles	0	0	2	5	0	2	1	0	0	8
Pirates	1	2	0	0	0	1	0	0	0	4

Baltimore	ab	r	h	bi	Pittsburgh	ab	r	h	bi
Garcia, ss	4	2	4	4	Moreno, cf	4	1	2	0
Ayala, lf	2	1	2	2	Foli, ss	4	0	0	0
Bumbry, cf	2	1	1	0	Parker, rf	3	0	0	1
Singleton, rf	5	0	2	1	B.Robinson, lf	4	0	1	0
Murray, 1b	4	0	0	0	Stargell, 1b	4	2	2	0
DeCinces, 3b	5	0	0	1	Madlock, 3b	4	0	1	1
Roenicke, cf	5	0	1	0	Nicosia, c	4	1	1	0
Dauer, 2b	5	1	1	0	Garner, 2b	4	0	1	2
Dempsey, c	5	2	2	0	Candelaria, p	1	0	1	0
McGregor, p	3	1	0	0	Romo, p	1	0	0	0
					Jackson, p	0	0	0	0
					Lacy, ph	1	0	0	0
					Tekulve, p	0	0	0	0
Totals	**40**	**8**	**13**	**8**		**34**	**4**	**9**	**4**

Errors: Foli, Stargell; 2B: Garcia, Moreno 2, Garner, Dauer, Stargell, Dempsey; 3B: Garcia; HR: Ayala

Baltimore Pitching	IP	H	R	ER	BB	SO
McGregor (W)	9	9	4	4	0	6
Pittsburgh Pitching						
Candelaria (L)	3	8	6	5	2	2
Romo	3 2/3	5	2	2	1	4
Jackson	1/3	0	0	0	0	0
Tekulve	2	0	0	0	0	1

Scott McGregor settled into his groove and retired the last 11 Pirates he faced with relative ease to ice the 8-4 victory, sending to their homes the disappointed fans who remained in the stadium until the bitter end.

Willie Stargell, who spent an hour answering reporters' questions following the Bucs' 3-2 victory the day before, reflected the mood of his teammates: "I'm not going to stay for an hour today. We played bad. Tell everyone else that, too."

Candelaria's father, who had never before seen him pitch in a big-league game, made the trip to Pittsburgh from Puerto Rico. After the game, his father jokingly said to his disgruntled son: "Do you mean I came this far to see something like this?"

Outside the locker room, under the cold, damp Pittsburgh skies, many of the departing fans attempted to bolster their confidence by humming the strains of "We Are Fam-a-Lee." This time, however, their music seemed to lack the customary beat of passion.

WORLD SERIES GAME 4
October 13, 1979
Three Rivers Stadium • Pittsburgh, Pennsylvania

ONCE AGAIN THE PUBLIC ADDRESS SYSTEM at windy Three Rivers played "We Are Fam-a-Lee," and another packed house sang along. One energetic fan shouted in a voice loud enough to be heard above the celebration: "Nobody can stop us now!" Enthusiastic support came from every township throughout Allegheny County and the surrounding areas. Even a Roman Catholic priest earlier that Saturday morning offered a public prayer in a downtown church asking the Lord that the Pirates tie the series at two games apiece.

Local fans of every faith truly believed these prayers would be answered when, in the home half of the second inning, Willie Stargell sent one of his patented drives skyrocketing over the right-center field wall for a 1-0 Pirates lead.

Reserve outfielder John Milner followed with a single. Bill Madlock and Ed Ott each hit book-rule doubles. Before the end of the inning, Scrap Iron Garner singled and reached second when Ott was caught in a rundown between third and home. Sammy Stewart replaced starting pitcher Dennis Martinez. Following an out, Omar Moreno singled home Garner. The home team enjoyed what looked like an insurmountable 4-0 lead. It appeared that the Pirates' ship was back on course.

Pirate starter Jim Bibby may have become overconfident as he allowed three Baltimore runners to cross the plate on a throwing error by Madlock, a single by Al Bumbry, a double by the hard-hitting Kiko Garcia and Ken Singleton's double. Bibby, however, bore down and kept the Orioles from scoring again.

Grant Jackson relieved Bibby with one out in the fifth and kept the Orioles at bay during that chilling October afternoon.

Reliever Steve Stone issued a walk to Tim Foli, Dave Parker singled and Milner doubled to give the Bucs another run in their half of the fifth. One inning later, Foli singled and crossed the plate when Willie Stargell doubled, giving the Pirates a comfortable 6-3 edge.

In the top of the eighth, with only six outs to go, the roof above the outfield seats at Three Rivers Stadium caved in. At least it seemed that way to the Pirate faithful watching from the stands or on television. Garcia looped a single to right, Singleton lined another one to left, and DeCinces walked to load the bases with one out. Chuck Tanner summoned from the bullpen his ace right-hander, Kent Tekulve. The electronic scoreboard above the center field wall flashed the message: "How do you spell relief? TEKULVE." This time, unfortunately, the "Tekulve magic" vanished. Pinch-hit, two-run doubles by John Lowenstein and Terry Crowley, plus the first major-league hit by rookie pitcher Tim Stoddard, added up to give Baltimore six runs.

When the dust finally cleared and echoes of the last faint cheer by a Bucs fan faded into dead silence, the Pirates had racked up a total of 17 hits, but they still were on the short end of a 9-6 Orioles comeback victory. Baltimore's clutch hitting prevailed, as the Pirates wasted a myriad of scoring opportunities.

After the contest, reporters wondered what happened to the ability of "Lumber and Lightning" to hit in the clutch as they had seen all season long. Dave Parker simply responded, "We just haven't been playing the kind of ball we're capable of."

The Pirates, now down three games to one, were but 27 outs away from losing the Series.

Game 4
Time: 3:48 • Attendance: 50,883

	1	2	3	4	5	6	7	8	9	R
Orioles	0	0	3	0	0	0	0	6	0	9
Pirates	0	4	0	0	1	1	0	0	0	6

Baltimore	ab	r	h	bi	Pittsburgh	ab	r	h	bi
Bumbry, cf	5	1	1	1	Moreno, cf	5	0	2	1
Garcia, ss	5	2	2	2	Foli, ss	4	2	3	0
Singleton, rf	5	0	3	1	Parker, rf	5	0	2	1
Murray, 1b	5	1	0	0	Stargell, 1b	5	1	3	1
DeCinces, 3b	1	1	0	0	Milner, lf	3	1	2	1
Roenicke, lf	3	0	0	0	D.Robinson, p	0	0	0	0
Lowenstein, lf	2	1	1	2	Tekulve, p	0	0	0	0
Dauer, 2b	3	0	1	0	Easler, ph	1	0	0	0
Smith, 2b	0	1	0	0	Madlock, 3b	3	1	2	0
Skaggs, c	3	1	1	0	Ott, c	5	0	1	2
Crowley, ph	1	0	1	2	Garner, 2b	4	1	2	0
Dempsey, c	0	1	0	0	Bibby, p	2	0	0	0
D. Martinez, p	0	0	0	0	Jackson, p	0	0	0	0
Stewart, p	1	0	0	0	B.Robinson, lf	1	0	0	0
May, ph	1	0	0	0					
Stone, p	0	0	0	0					
Kelly, ph	1	0	1	0					
Stoddard, p	1	0	1	1					
Totals	**37**	**9**	**12**	**9**		**38**	**6**	**17**	**6**

Error: Madlock; DP: Baltimore 2, Pittsburgh 3; 2B: Madlock, Ott, Garcia, Singleton, Stargell, Parker, Lowenstein; HR: Stargell; SB: DeCinces

Baltimore Pitching	IP	H	R	ER	BB	SO
D. Martinez	1 1/3	6	4	4	0	0
Stewart	2 2/3	4	0	0	1	0
Stone	2	4	2	2	2	2
Stoddard (W)	3	3	0	0	1	3
Pittsburgh Pitching						
Bibby	6 1/3	7	3	2	2	7
Jackson	2/3	0	0	0	0	0
D. Robinson	1/3	2	3	3	1	0
Tekulve (L)	1 2/3	3	3	3	2	1

About 250 miles to the east, *Baltimore Sun* editors searched bins housing large enough letters for war-size headlines that would announce:"World Champions!"The Orioles were putting on a base-ball clinic, and it seemed as though all the Pirates could do was to stand by and watch.

Even the normally optimistic Tekulve sat in the clubhouse star-ing at the floor and apologizing to his teammates for letting them down.

Could it be that the Fam-a-Lee was ready to split up?

WORLD SERIES GAME 5
October 14, 1979
Three Rivers Stadium • Pittsburgh, Pennsylvania

A **PALL HUNG** over the Pittsburgh Pirates locker room on that Sunday afternoon. Not only were the Pirates on the brink of elimi-nation from World Series play; of far greater significance was anoth-er bit of bad news.

Manager Chuck Tanner, normally smiling and upbeat, sat alone behind his office desk, starring into space. He had just received the word that nearly every son eventually hears: his beloved mother, Anna, had died a few hours earlier.

Refusing to allow even this personal tragedy to interfere with his team's slim chances of winning the World Series, Tanner insisted on remaining at the helm. "My mother would have wanted me to do just that," he said.

Outside, the majority of the 50,920 Pirate fans who passed through the turnstiles on the afternoon of Sunday, October 14, were unaware of the personal tragedy that weighed on Tanner's shoulders. Their concerns focused on the Bucs. Meanwhile, the players became more determined. "We can do it for Chuck's Mom," said Grant Jackson.

In spite of the current status of the Series, the support of the entire city for its team never waned. The downtown Alcoa Building had "Beat 'em Bucs" spelled out in its windows. Spectators clapped in rhythm when the loud speakers of Three Rivers again belted out the recording by Sister Sledge: "We Are Fam-a-Lee!" A white sheet hung on the outfield wall with a hand-painted note of encouragement: "Never Say Die!" One especially optimistic fan from suburban Bridgeville was interviewed on national television and boldly proclaimed: "The Orioles? We're gonna pluck 'em tonight, cook 'em the next game and eat 'em in the last game." Even a Lutheran pastor from nearby Johnstown in his sermon that morning predicted that the Pirates would prevail when he jokingly pointed to a passage in the Bible—Genesis 1:28: ". . . and he shall have dominion over the birds."

Amid all the shouting and optimism, inside the hearts and minds of every Pittsburgh fan was a hard, cold reality that equaled the chilling outside temperature. The fact nobody could deny was that the Pirates were down three games to one. Even if the Bucs should win tonight's contest, they had to return for the final two games of the Series to the not-so-friendly venue known as Baltimore's Memorial Stadium.

Baseball writer Kenneth Shouler recalls, "With the Birds up three games to one, I remember telling my father that they couldn't lose, especially with pitchers such as Palmer, McGregor and Flanagan still to pitch."

Some Las Vegas bookmakers labeled the Pirates as 100-to-1 underdogs.

Logical thinking notwithstanding, when former Pirate hero Bill Mazeroski—the man who struck the memorable home run to win the World Series against the mighty New York Yankees in 1960—was introduced to throw out the first pitch, fans and players alike cheered with hope. Maybe ... maybe ... miracles can still happen on a Pittsburgh baseball diamond.

Before the game, two other things inspired the Pirates to play with even more determination. In the clubhouse that morning was a copy of the Sunday edition of the *Baltimore Sun*. The headline told of a plan announced by Baltimore mayor William Donald Schaefer of the route for a parade the next morning to welcome home the "World Champion Orioles." "When we saw that," said Kent Tekulve, "we knew we not only wanted to win the game, we wanted to cancel their parade."

The second motivating factor was a news clipping posted on the message board telling that Oriole catcher Rick Dempsey had already made plans on how he was going to spend his "winner's share" of the World Series money. "That, too, spurred us on," said Tekulve.

Thirty seven-year-old Jim Rooker (with a modest 4-7 record and eight weeks on the disabled list that year) was Manager Tanner's rather bizarre selection to start this crucial game for the Bucs; Mike Flanagan, Baltimore's ace and winner of Game 1, started for the Birds.

On paper, the pitching selections escalated the apprehension of Pirate fans. But Rooker's slider was exceptionally sharp that evening. He tossed four innings of no-hit ball, allowing only one run in the top of the fifth. Meanwhile, Flanagan did even better by serving up "goose eggs" for five full innings.

After reliever Bert Blyleven, who possessed what was probably the greatest curveball in the National League, blanked the Orioles in the top of the sixth, Flanagan appeared to lose a touch of his domination. He walked Tim Foli. Dave Parker's single sent Foli to second. Bill Robinson's sacrifice bunt advanced both runners. Foli scored and Parker trudged into third on Willie Stargell's sacrifice fly. A clutch RBI single by Bill Madlock—one of his four hits that afternoon—gave the Bucs a 2-1 lead.

The Pirates finally broke loose with a barrage of hits that must have appeared to be shot out of a machine gun to Oriole relievers Tim Stoddard, Tippy Martinez and Don Stanhouse. Garner singled, Foli tripled and Parker doubled for two more runs in the seventh. Eighth-inning singles by Stargell, Madlock, Garner and Foli produced three more runs.

"That did not surprise me," said Dave Parker. "Our hitting was contagious. When one player started to hit, everyone else followed suit."

The electronic scoreboard at Three Rivers flashed a message that expressed the feelings of everyone at the ballpark that evening: "Unbelievable!" Once again, the stadium erupted with what now became both a love song and a fight song, "We Are Fam-a-Lee!"

Blyleven, in his first relief appearance in seven years, earned the awe even of Kent Tekulve as he shut out the Birds the rest of the way.

The final score was Pittsburgh 7, Baltimore 1.

Newly adopted Fam-a-Lee members Tim Foli and Bill Madlock both deserved the spotlight as the former Mets shortstop drove in

Game 5
Time: 2:54 • Attendance: 50,920

	1	2	3	4	5	6	7	8	9	R
Orioles	0	0	0	0	1	0	0	0	0	1
Pirates	0	0	0	0	0	2	2	3	x	7

Baltimore	ab	r	h	bi	Pittsburgh	ab	r	h	bi
Garcia, ss	4	0	0	0	Moreno, cf	4	1	0	0
Ayala, lf	1	0	0	0	Foli, ss	4	2	2	3
Bumbry, cf	1	0	0	0	Parker, rf	4	1	2	1
Singleton, rf	4	0	0	0	B.Robinson, lf	4	0	1	0
Murray, 1b	4	0	0	0	Stargell, 1b	3	1	1	1
Roenicke, cf	4	1	1	0	Madlock, 3b	4	1	4	1
DeCinces, 3b	4	0	2	0	Nicosia, c	4	0	0	0
Dauer, 2b	3	0	0	0	Garner, 2b	4	1	2	1
Lowenstein, ph	1	0	1	0	Rooker, p	1	0	0	0
Dempsey, c	3	0	2	0	Lacy, ph	1	0	1	0
Crowley, ph	1	0	0	0	Blyleven, p	1	0	0	0
Flanagan, p	1	0	0	0					
Kelly, ph	1	0	0	0					
Stoddard, p	0	0	0	0					
T. Martinez, p	0	0	0	0					
Stanhouse, p	0	0	0	0					
Totals	**32**	**1**	**6**	**0**		**34**	**7**	**13**	**7**

Errors: Garner, Stoddard, Stanhouse; DP: Pittsburgh 2; 2B: B. Robinson, Roenicke, Dempsey, Parker; 3B: Foli

Baltimore Pitching	IP	H	R	ER	BB	SO
Flanagan (L)	6	6	2	2	1	6
Stoddard	2/3	2	2	2	0	0
T. Martinez	1/3	2	1	1	0	0
Stanhouse	1	3	2	2	2	0
Pittsburgh Pitching						
Rooker	5	3	1	1	2	2
Blyleven (W)	4	3	0	0	1	3

three runs and the muscular third baseman went four for four. There was no arguing that a Fam-a-Lee feeling was coming back.

Captain Willie Stargell summarized the commitment of his team: "In this game, you have to have as much courage as talent."

More than ever before in his life, manager Chuck Tanner knew this was true.

WORLD SERIES GAME 6
October 16, 1979
Memorial Stadium • Baltimore, Maryland

ON THE FLIGHT to Baltimore, the Pirates were exceptionally loose. John Candelaria walked onto the airplane wearing a Baltimore Orioles hat. Manager Tanner pretended not to notice it. By the time the plane landed at Baltimore, the Pirates were reminding one another with the utmost confidence: "We know we can win this thing."

"It was over with," said Scrap Iron.

Jim Rooker agreed. "It was just a matter of time."

Pirate equipment manager John Hallahan reminded the players to bring down their luggage to the lobby before the game in the event the team would have to leave Baltimore that evening. Candelaria refused. "I'm pitching tonight. Why should I bring my suitcase downstairs? We're going to be here at least one more night."

The previously arctic weather had suddenly turned balmy the next day, but that seemed to be of little help to Candelaria (loser of Game 3) who was still ailing from a sore back and aching ribs. He promised manager Tanner that he would go as far as his body would allow on that night of October 16. He knew, as did his teammates and the millions of Pirate supporters back in Pittsburgh and throughout America, that the team faced a seemingly insurmountable task—to win two more games against the Baltimore Orioles in Memorial Stadium. The Candy Man, however, was determined to give whatever he had left for his Fam-a-Lee.

He looked as though he didn't have much in the first inning when Baltimore put two men on with only one out. A quick double play snuffed out a potential rally.

The two starting pitchers—Candelaria and Baltimore's Jim Palmer—controlled the game. Through six innings, the Candy Man had allowed six hits and no walks; Palmer, who looked unbeatable just as the scouts and oddsmakers predicted, gave up only four hits and no walks.

With no score, Omar Moreno opened the Bucs' half of the seventh with a "seeing eye" ground-ball single that rolled between first and second, just beyond the outstretched glove of Eddie Murray. While good contact hitter Tim Foli stood at the plate, Moreno took off for second on a hit-and-run play. Foli hit a bouncer up the middle that just ticked Palmer's glove and might have been turned into a double play, but the speedy Moreno was already sliding into second by the time shortstop Kiko Garcia got to the grounder. Garcia looked distracted by the oncoming Moreno and paused for a fraction of a second. That's all it took. He snapped the ball to first much too late. Both runners were safe. Although the official ruling was a "hit," everyone who saw it knew it was a mental misplay.

Left-handed-hitting Dave Parker rapped a bad-hop single that knuckled past second baseman Rich Dauer bringing home Moreno for the first run, while Foli moved to third. Willie Stargell's sacrifice fly scored the Bucco shortstop.

With one out in the top of the eighth, Ed Ott singled and Phil Garner hit a ground-rule double. A sacrifice fly by Bill Robinson brought home Ott with run number three. Moreno followed with a single scoring Garner; it was his seventh hit in the last four games.

Tekulve, employing his maddening "whirlybird" sinkers, preserved Candelaria's shutout throughout the final three innings, retiring the last seven batters in order, four by strikeout. Both Bucs pitchers earned their "stars" this game.

The 4-0 victory tied the fall classic at three games each.

Could it be that Pittsburgh fans would witness another miracle?

Was the Fam-a-Lee destined to become a legend?

"Whatever we were to become," said Tekulve, "we knew one thing: We cancelled their crummy parade for at least one more day."

Game 6
Time: 2:30 • Attendance: 53,739

	1	2	3	4	5	6	7	8	9	R
Pirates	0	0	0	0	0	0	2	2	0	4
Orioles	0	0	0	0	0	0	0	0	0	0

Pittsburgh	ab	r	h	bi	Baltimore	ab	r	h	bi
Moreno, cf	5	1	3	1	Garcia, ss	3	0	1	0
Foli, ss	5	1	2	0	Kelly, ph	1	0	0	0
Parker, rf	4	0	1	1	Belanger, ss	0	0	0	0
Stargell, 1b	4	0	0	1	Ayala, lf	3	0	0	0
Milner, lf	3	0	0	0	Crowley, ph	1	0	0	0
Tekulve, p	1	0	0	0	Stoddard, p	0	0	0	0
Madlock, 3b	3	0	0	0	Singleton, rf	4	0	3	0
Ott, c	4	1	2	0	Murray, 1b	4	0	0	0
Garner, 2b	3	1	2	0	DeCinces, 3b	4	0	0	0
Candelaria, p	2	0	0	0	Roenicke, cf	2	0	0	0
B. Robinson, ph	0	0	0	1	Bumbry, cf	1	0	0	0
					Dauer, 2b	2	0	1	0
					Smith, 2b	1	0	1	0
					Dempsey, c	3	0	1	0
					Palmer, p	2	0	0	0
					Lowenstein, lf	1	0	0	0
Totals	**35**	**4**	**10**	**4**		**32**	**0**	**7**	**0**

Error: Bumbry; DP: Pirates 2; 2B: Foli, Garner

Pittsburgh Pitching	IP	H	R	ER	BB	SO
Candelaria (W)	6	6	0	0	0	2
Tekulve (S)	3	0	0	0	0	4
Baltimore Pitching						
Palmer (L)	8	10	4	4	3	4
Stoddard	1	0	0	0	0	0

WORLD SERIES GAME 7
"The Clincher"

October 17, 1979
Memorial Stadium • Baltimore, Maryland

DAVID FINOLI AND Bill Rainer, authors of *The Pittsburgh Pirates Encyclopedia*, label Game 7 of the 1979 World Series as the fourth best game in the history of the ball club. Some astute Pirate fans might challenge their ranking, yet nobody could deny that this matchup between the Bucs and the Baltimore Orioles was, by far, the most important game of the year. After all, this one was for all the marbles.

On that memorable October 17, the front page of *The Pittsburgh Press* read: One More Time, Maestro, If You Please."

Just four days earlier, sportswriters around the nation had written their obituaries for the Pittsburgh Pirates, when the Steel City team was down three games to one to the powerful Orioles.

The Bucs refused to raise their arms in surrender. They bested Earl Weaver's squad, 7-1, in Game 4—their last appearance that year at Three Rivers. But with Baltimore's 3-2 advantage, these same sportswriters considered it only a matter of time before the American League Champions would capture the flag. The fact that at the last two games of the Series would be played in the hostile environment (at least to Pirate fans) of Memorial Stadium support-ed that belief.

John Candelaria and his Pirates may not have read the newspa-pers that day. Hence, they didn't know that the Orioles had an insur-mountable lead. Behind the solid seven-hit pitching of the Candy Man and Kent Tekulve, the Bucs shut out future Hall of Famer Jim Palmer and the Orioles, 4-0, to tie the Series at three games apiece.

Now it was October 17, 1979—"D-Day."

Preparations on both sides intensified. Every player, coach and manager searched inside himself for an edge.

If there was an edge in confidence, it had to belong to the Bucs. "Heck," said Candelaria, "we've already cancelled two parades. Let's go win this thing!"

Manager Chuck Tanner selected hard-throwing right-hander Jim Bibby to start Game 7. The Orioles' Scott McGregor, an effective southpaw with excellent control, was his mound opponent.

The now-traditional pregame gyrations by "Wild Bill" Hagy were followed by president Jimmy Carter, the first president to attend the fall classic since Dwight Eisenhower in 1956. President Carter tossed out the ceremonial first pitch in front of 53,733 enthusiastic Oriole fans and the largest television audience ever to watch a World Series game. This final contest was played in a pleasant 65 degrees—by far the best weather conditions for the entire Series.

Second baseman Rich Dauer, a .257 hitter with only 43 homers in a 10-year major-league career and with never more than nine home runs in any given season, made a genuine bid to become a household name when he lined a shot into the left-field stands in the bottom of the third to put the Orioles up, 1-0. The volume of cheering Oriole fans increased as they mentally prepared for what they thought was an overdue downtown victory parade.

Although he admitted that this was the best game he had ever seen Bibby pitch, manager Tanner needed some runs, so he pinch hit for Bibby in the top of the fifth. The move, however, failed to get his Bucs on the board. Still trailing by one run, the Pirates sent Don Robinson to the hill to begin the home half of the inning. Robinson, whose shoulder was aching more than at any time during the season, got two outs, then showed a streak of wildness when he yielded a single and walked the opposing pitcher, McGregor. Tanner then called in left-hander Grant Jackson, who was able to retire the side.

Pittsburgh managed only three hits off the lefty McGregor until the top half of the sixth when, with one out, Bill Robinson, another late-blooming Pirate veteran, grounded a bullet past the reach of shortstop Kiko Garcia for a single.

With Baltimore fans counting the outs remaining for a victory, the stage was set for the man whom *The Sporting News* would name "Major League Player of the Year"—Willie Stargell. The Pirate captain had already racked up two tainted hits that game—a bloop single to left and a bloop double to the same spot, both when he appeared to be fooled by McGregor's off-speed pitches. Stargell, who had hit the only two home runs for his team during the Series, this time patiently waited for the first pitch from McGregor—a low, inside slider. The man showed why he was worth his weight in "Stargell Stars" when he swung and "golfed" a fly ball to deep right-center field. Outfielder Ken Singleton ran to the fence, jumped, and reached as high as his 6'4" frame allowed. His glove was a few inches short, and the ball landed out of sight. As Singleton's left arm remained draped over the fence, Stargell rounded the bases to score the go-ahead run for Pittsburgh.

Memorial Stadium fell silent. The mourning had begun.

Grant Jackson, unscored upon in the Series, kept Oriole bats quiet in their halves of the sixth and seventh innings. In the bottom of the eighth, with the Pirates still leading 2-1, Jackson showed signs of tiring as, with one out, he walked the first two batters. Tanner then signaled for his ace, Kent Tekulve. The 6' 4" slender side-armer had responded so well in similar situations throughout the regular season, but he now faced what was perhaps his greatest challenge all season. On deck was a most formidable lineup of hitters—pinch hitter Terry Crowley (who had smacked a game-winning double off Tekulve in Game 4), Singleton (who led all Baltimore batters with 10 hits in the Series), and, if either of his teammates reached base, slugger Eddie Murray.

Crowley hit a slow grounder to second for the second out, but both runners advanced into scoring position.

The Baltimore faithful cheered with increased enthusiasm when Tekulve walked Singleton. As if scripted by the baseball gods who seem to do this many times, Eddie Murray dug his cleats into the dirt of the batter's box. Murray, however, was not at the top of his game during this Series, going 0 for his last 20 times at bat. Tekulve threw a sinker on the outside of the plate. Murray swung hard, but got under it and sent a fly ball to deep right. Dave Parker started in for the ball, but slipped slightly.

Pirate fans watching on television gasped. The silence of the Oriole fans was broken by a spontaneous cheer. Parker recovered in plenty of time to make an easy catch for the final out of the inning. Once again, Memorial Stadium became a mausoleum.

In the top of the ninth, manager Earl Weaver used a World Series-record five different pitchers in an attempt to keep the game close. Weaver, who had earned a reputation as an unorthodox manager, decided this time to play things "by the book." Conventional strategy, however, backfired. With Tim Stoddard on the mound in relief, Garner doubled. With one out, Mike Flanagan (the winningest pitcher in the majors that season) served up a single to Omar Moreno that scored Garner. Weaver followed the sage advice of bringing in right-handed pitchers to face right-handed batters, and vice versa. Don Stanhouse relieved Flanagan, and Foli greeted him with a single to center that got Moreno to third. The Baltimore manager called in from the bullpen southpaw Tippy Martinez to pitch to left-handed-hitting Dave Parker. Martinez promptly hit

Omar Moreno had a helluva series, finishing with eleven hits and the distinction of catching the final out.

Parker to load the bases. Applying the same conservative approach, Weaver summoned a right-hander, Dennis Martinez (no relation to Tippy), to pitch to right-handed-swinging Bill Robinson. Robinson was also hit with a pitch, thereby forcing in an unorthodox second insurance run for the Pirates.

With the score at a more comfortable 4-1 in his favor, Tekulve laid the Orioles to rest when he struck out the first two batters of the inning on just six sliders, all of which were wide of the strike zone. When Tekulve got the ball back from catcher Steve Nicosia, he casually walked over to third-baseman Mad Dog Madlock and quietly said, "When we started spring training, 28 teams looked for the last out of the World Series. We're going to find that out right now."

With that, Teke calmly returned to the mound and laid the Orioles to rest when Baltimore pinch hitter Pat Kelly lofted a lazy fly ball into the waiting glove of outfielder Omar Moreno. Tekulve, who had earlier promised himself that he would not make a foolish display if he was on the mound for the final out, forgot that pledge. He leaped high off the mound, stretched his arms skyward and let out a shout of celebration.

So did every Pirates fan.

It may have been a childlike display of emotions, but world champions are permitted to do that.

In Pittsburgh, the cry went out: "Our Fam-a-Lee has just won its fifth World Series in franchise history."

As announcer Lanny Frattare would have said: "There was noooooooooooooooo doubt about it!"

SAME SERIES; DIFFERENT VIEW

MICHAEL R. CONNER of Baltimore worked for the Orioles at Memorial Stadium for 15 seasons. He tells the story of how the '79 Series had a special impact upon him:

"I used to work for a while as an usher behind the visitors' dugout, which would be section 39. From our viewpoint, one could look straight down the left field line into the 309 corner. The right field corner was always hidden from us, but there were some crazy

Game 7

Time: 2:54 • Attendance: 53,733

	1	2	3	4	5	6	7	8	9	R
Pirates	0	0	0	0	0	2	0	0	2	4
Orioles	0	0	1	0	0	0	0	0	0	1

Pittsburgh	ab	r	h	bi	Baltimore	ab	r	h	bi
Moreno, cf	5	1	3	1	Bumbry, cf	3	0	0	0
Foli, ss	4	0	1	0	Garcia, ss	3	0	1	0
Parker, rf	4	0	0	0	Ayala, ph	0	0	0	0
B. Robinson, lf	4	1	1	1	Crowley, ph	1	0	0	0
Stargell, 1b	5	1	4	2	Stoddard, p	0	0	0	0
Madlock, 3b	3	0	0	0	Flanagan, p	0	0	0	0
Nicosia, c	4	0	0	0	Stanhouse, p	0	0	0	0
Garner, 2b	3	1	1	0	T. Martinez, p	0	0	0	0
Bibby, p	1	0	0	0	D. Martinez, p	0	0	0	0
Sanguillen, ph	1	0	0	0	Singleton, rf	3	0	0	0
D. Robinson, p	0	0	0	0	Murray, 1b	4	0	0	0
Jackson, p	1	0	0	0	Lowenstein, lf	2	0	0	0
Tekulve, p	1	0	0	0	Roenicke, lf	2	0	0	0
					DeCinces, 3b	4	0	2	0
					Dempsey, c	3	0	0	0
					Kelly, ph	1	0	0	0
					Dauer, 2b	3	1	1	1
					McGregor, p	1	0	0	0
					May, ph	0	0	0	0
					Belanger, ss	0	0	0	0
Totals	36	4	10	4		30	1	4	1

Errors: Lowenstein, Garcia; DP: Orioles 1; 2B: Stargell 2, Garner; HR: Dauer, Stargell

Pittsburgh Pitching	IP	H	R	ER	BB	SO
Bibby	4	3	1	1	0	3
D. Robinson	2/3	1	0	0	1	0
Jackson (W)	2 2/3	0	0	0	2	1
Tekulve (S)	1 2/3	0	0	0	1	1
Baltimore Pitching						
McGregor (L)	8	7	2	2	2	2
Stoddard	1/3	1	1	1	0	0
Flanagan	0	1	1	1	0	0
Stanhouse	0	1	0	0	0	0
T. Martinez	0	0	0	0	0	0
D. Martinez	2/3	0	0	0	0	0

caroms as would-be doubles turned into triples when the ball would strike the angled doorway. It was behind this where the grounds crew kept supplies such as sand for rain-soaked mounds.

"My memory was of the night where I worked the final game of the 1979 World Series between the Orioles and the Pittsburgh Pirates. After Willie Stargell's homer, the fans sensed doom. You could read it on their faces. When the Pirates scored two runs in the ninth, there was a mass exodus like I've never seen. Pirate wives were standing in the aisle, and black and gold was pervasive. My instructions were not to allow anyone onto the dugout or onto the field after the completion of the game. When the Orioles' Pat Kelly flew out, the Pittsburgh crowd erupted, and wives, friends and Pirate fans stood en masse, disco-dancing on the dugout to the song "We Are Fam-a-Lee." These concrete structures had no support beams, and I began to panic. Shouting to be heard, I implored the fans to get off the dugout. A Pirate wife, Mrs. Moreno, I believe, said to me, 'Don't worry, honey. We got lots of insurance.'

"Leaving them to their celebration, I retreated into the cavernous underground of the stadium. There was a labyrinth of passages, some leading to the clubhouses, some to Oriole offices. I passed a delirious Kent Tekulve, who had quaffed a split of celebratory champagne, when the networks had sent someone to interview him. A couple of Pirate office personnel had his arms around their necks as they escorted/dragged him to the awaiting TV audience. He seemed barely able to utter monosyllabic responses. How he carried it off for TV is a wonderment to me.

"Going back to the break room to return my uniform, I encountered a beaming man dressed in a Pirate uniform. He turned around to pat some of the celebrating pitchers on the back (It had spilled into our room by this time), and I saw on his uniform the name Haddix. It was Pirate pitching coach Harvey Haddix. He turned and beheld me, his countenance radiant and a hint of moisture in his eyes. I said congratulations to him. He shook my hand vigorously and said, 'Thank you so much. Oh, what a thrill.'

"I asked him if the 12-inning perfect game might have topped this.

"'Oh no,' he said. 'This was so much better. These were my guys.'"

A Dream Come True

KENT TEKULVE, CALLED "Teke" by many of his teammates, said the conclusion of the seventh game of the World Series was the pinnacle of his career. "There's no better feeling in the world," he still says. "Millions and millions of kids dreamt that dream and I was one of the few that got to live it."

Tekulve would savor that feeling even more after he retired. He knew that the World Series victory was not the beginning of a dynasty. Instead, it marked the end of a glorious era.

Now, That's a Tip!

THE PIRATES WERE obviously a very generous Fam-a-Lee. They voted to give a one-quarter share of the World Series money to each of the youngsters who worked so faithfully in the clubhouse all year. Batboys Steve Graff and Steve Hallahan, plus assistant clubhouse custodian Gary Hallahan, each received $7,000. That was a whopping sum, especially when you compared it to most teams—including the wealthy New York Yankees—who only gave a $500 bonus to their clubhouse staff.

Head clubhouse man John Hallahan and trainer Tony Bartirome also received full shares.

Other Reasons to Celebrate the 1979 World Series

• WILLIE STARGELL, WINNER of the World Series MVP Award, tied for the National League MVP Award. He was also named MVP for the League Championship Series, winner of *Sports Illustrated*'s "Co-Man of the Year Award" (along with the Steelers' Terry Bradshaw), and winner of *The Sporting News* "Major League Player of the Year."

He was, at age 39, the oldest man ever to win any of these honors. In fact, he was the only man ever to win all of these awards in one season.

• Of Willie Stargell's 12 hits, the seven of the extra-base variety set a World Series record.

• The Pirates' team batting average of .323 was the highest ever for a World Series winner. That was nearly 100 points higher than the .232 average of the Orioles.

• Dave Parker racked up 10 Series hits.

• So did Tim Foli.

• Although he started slowly with only one hit in 10 at-bats, Omar Moreno ended the Series with 11 hits, just one short of the Series record.

• Bill Madlock batted .375.

• Phil "Scrap Iron" Garner got 12 hits in 24 at-bats for an astounding .500 average. He joined Pepper Martin (St. Louis Cardinals, 1931) and Johnny Lindell (New York Yankees, 1947) as the only players to bat .500 in seven World Series games. In a sense he "warmed up" for the fall classic by batting a torrid .417 in the National League Championship Series. These figures, coupled with his career-high .293 average during the regular season made 1979 a season to remember.

• Tim Foli, in 33 trips to the plate, did not strike out once. That, too, remains a World Series record.

• For the benefit of those baseball fans who are fascinated with rare statistics, one rather obscure record was set during the top half of the ninth inning of Game 7 of the World Series. Baltimore's southpaw reliever, Tippy Martinez, faced Pirate slugger Dave Parker. Martinez plunked Parker with a fastball, awarding the Bucs' right-fielder first base, loading the bases. The Orioles' next pitcher, Dennis Martinez, hit the next Pirate hitter (Bill Robinson) to force in a run. Here comes the bit of baseball trivia that's sure to win you a wager or two: This was the only time in World Series history that there were two hit batsmen in a row by two unrelated pitchers having the same surname. Now that's a record that should stand for centuries.

• Here's another one. Although the speedy Pirates stole 180 bases during the regular season, they swiped none in the Series. That, of course, ties a record as well.

• Relief pitcher Kent Tekulve set a Series record in 1979 when he recorded three saves. In reality, however, the lanky southpaw only tied a record that was set 19 years earlier by another Pirate—Elroy Face. Although Face could have been given credit for three saves during the Bucs' memorable Series against Mickey Mantle, Roger Maris and the heavily favored New York Yankees, in 1960 saves were not considered an official statistic until 1969.

• Pittsburgh's pitching staff held the Orioles to an embarrassing two runs in the final 28 innings of the Series.

• The Pittsburgh Steelers would go on to win another Super Bowl, thus making Pittsburgh the undisputed "City of Champions." As a result of these victories and their leadership, both Willie Stargell and quarterback Terry Bradshaw of the Steelers were selected as the first dual "Sportsmen of the Year" by *Sports Illustrated*.

Pirates World Series Statistics

Player:	Avg.	AB	R	H	2B	3B	HR	RBI	SB
Matt Alexander, of	.000	0	0	0	0	0	0	0	0
Jim Bibby, p	.000	4	0	0	0	0	0	0	0
Bert Blyleven, p	.000	3	0	0	0	0	0	0	0
John Candelaria, p	.333	3	0	1	0	0	0	0	0
Mike Easler, ph	.000	1	0	0	0	0	0	0	0
Tim Foli, ss	.333	30	6	10	1	1	0	3	0
Phil Garner, 2b	.500	24	4	12	4	0	0	5	0
Grant Jackson, p	.000	1	0	0	0	0	0	0	0
Bruce Kison, p	.000	0	0	0	0	0	0	0	0
Lee Lacy, ph	.250	4	0	1	0	0	0	0	0
Bill Madlock, 3b	.375	24	2	9	1	0	0	3	0
John Milner, of	.333	9	2	3	1	0	0	1	0
Omar Moreno, of	.333	33	4	11	2	0	0	3	0
Steve Nicosia, c	.062	16	1	1	0	0	0	0	0
Ed Ott, c	.333	12	2	4	1	0	0	3	0
Dave Parker, of	.345	29	2	10	3	0	0	4	0
Don Robinson, p	.000	0	0	0	0	0	0	0	0
Bill Robinson, of	.263	19	2	5	1	0	0	2	0
Enrique Romo, p	.000	1	0	0	0	0	0	0	0
Jim Rooker, p	.000	2	0	0	0	0	0	0	0
Manny Sanguillen, ph	.333	3	0	1	0	0	0	1	0
Willie Stargell, 1b	.400	30	7	12	4	0	3	7	0
Rennie Stennett, ph	1.000	1	0	1	0	0	0	0	0
Kent Tekulve, p	.000	2	0	0	0	0	0	0	0
Total	**.323**	**251**	**32**	**81**	**18**	**1**	**3**	**32**	**0**

Pitcher:	W	L	ERA	G	IP	H	ER	BB	SO
Jim Bibby	0	0	2.61	2	10.1	10	3	2	10
Bert Blyleven	1	0	1.80	2	10.0	8	2	3	4
John Candelaria	1	1	5.00	2	9.0	14	5	2	4
Grant Jackson	1	0	0.00	4	4.2	1	0	2	2
Bruce Kison	0	1	108.0	0	0.1	3	4	2	0
Don Robinson	1	0	5.40	4	5.0	4	3	6	3
Enrique Romo	0	0	3.86	2	4.2	5	2	3	4
Jim Rooker	0	0	1.04	2	8.2	5	1	3	4
Kent Tekulve	0	1	2.89	5	9.1	4	3	3	10
Total	**4**	**3**	**3.34**		**62.0**	**54**	**23**	**26**	**41**

CHAPTER NINE

AFTERGLOW

Sunset and evening star
And one clear call for me!
And may there be no moaning of the bar
When I put out to sea.

—*Tennyson*

ONE OF THE RICH REWARDS of a baseball fan is the storehouse of priceless memories he or she has about previous games and players of a bygone era. Long after the last out is called and the winter snows compel others to think of other things and other sports, the true baseball fan relives some of the great moments of the past season.

Attending a baseball game at PNC Park is, of course, a genuine treat. Sitting next to someone who is knowledgeable and being able to bask in the history of the sport is a bonus. A clutch hit, a daring steal, a powerful home run—all can trigger memories of former Pirates who gave spectacular performances on the field.

It may be said that the memories of events past, like good wine, become more delicious with time. Think back to those wonderful sights: a Kiner shot over the scoreboard at Forbes Field . . . a rifle throw by Clemente nailing an overconfident runner attempting to score on a fly ball to right . . . a grab of a toss by Maz at second followed by a lightning pivot to complete a double play. Each becomes a focal point in our lives.

May the stories in this book remind us of one special year, one special team, one special manager, one special captain, and, of course, one special Fam-a-Lee.

As a special farewell, here are a few related stories to add to the glow of the world champion 1979 Pittsburgh Pirates.

TRIBUTE BY THE PLAYERS

EACH OF THE 2001 PIRATES wore a two-and-a-half-inch black circle patch on both their home and road uniforms. The patch had a gold star (akin to a "Stargell Star") and a black "S" in honor of their beloved captain who died on April 9, 2004.

A NIGHT ON THE TOWN

JOE MORGAN, Hall of Fame second baseman who idolized Willie Stargell, recalls how he and the legendary Pirate slugger arranged to meet after a game in Pittsburgh to hit some of night spots. After several hours of "sociological study," Morgan and some of his teammates who joined them, insisted on returning to the hotel to rest for the next day's game.

"Stargell didn't return home until about eight in the morning," says Morgan. "Just a few hours later, Willie slammed two home runs and went five for five. I, on the other hand, got only one hit . . . on a bunt.

"On one of his trips around the bases after hitting a home run, Stargell passed me as I was standing near second base and said, 'Rest is overrated.'"

QUICK EXIT

GAME 1 OF THE NLCS in 1979 between Cincinnati and Pittsburgh at Riverfront Stadium was a memorable contest that's often replayed on "ESPN Classic." It was a close contest that featured starting pitchers Tom Seaver for the Reds and John Candelaria for the Pirates.

Although both pitchers did not have their best stuff, they were tough when it counted. In spite of yielding home runs to the Bucs' Phil Garner and Cincinnati's George Foster, each starter held the opposition to a mere two runs. Relievers Enrique Romo, Kent Tekulve and Grant Jackson kept the Reds in check.

With runners on first and second and no outs for Pittsburgh in the top of the 11th, Willie Stargell stepped to the plate. Cincinnati outfielders played so deep that they had paint on their backs. Even that didn't help. Stargell smacked a Tom Hume fastball high and long to center field. All Dave Collins could do was turn and watch in frustration as the ball sailed over the fence into the crowd.

Commenting on the nationally televised game that night for NBC Sports was former Pirate Joe Garagiola. He saw many of the 50,006 in attendance scurry to the exits of the ballpark and responded with one of his patented expressions: "The fans are leaving as if the stadium is on fire."

Later in the same NLCS (won by Pittsburgh in three straight games), the quick-witted former catcher noticed that a batted ball took a bad hop when it hit a seam in the stadium's artificial turf. "I never thought the day would come when the outcome of a game would be decided on the skills of a good tailor," he quipped.

Remarks such as these helped usher Garagiola (a nine-year veteran with a .257 career average) into the Writers'/ Broadcasters' Wing of the Hall of Fame in 1991.

No Quota System Here

Four players who appeared on the roster of the '79 world Champion Pittsburgh Pirates—Willie Stargell, Manny Sanguillen, Rennie Stennett and Dock Ellis—were parts of Major League Baseball history eight years earlier. On September 1, 1971 (during Pittsburgh's previous successful quest for a World Series Championship ring), Bucs manager Danny Murtaugh handed the lineup card to the home-plate umpire. On it was the starting lineup:

Rennie Stennett – Second Base
Gene Clines – Center Field
Roberto Clemente – Right Field
Willie Stargell – Left Field
Manny Sanguillen – Catcher
Dave Cash – Third Base
Al Oliver – First Base
Jackie Hernandez – Shortstop
Dock Ellis – Pitcher

What was different about this list? It was the first time a major league team had ever filled its starting lineup with all minority players.

Following the Pirates' 10-7 win that night over the Philadelphia Phillies, manager Murtaugh met with the scores of reporters who pressed against each other outside the Pirates' locker room eager to get a sound bite or two for the evening news or next morning's newspaper. One of the reporters, perhaps looking for a juicy story that would generate some controversy, challenged Murtaugh with a pointed question: "Why would you would use such a 'gimmick,' especially when your club is in the midst of a pennant race?"

Prior to hearing the question, Murtaugh had been oblivious to what he had done. In reacting to the reporter's challenging question, Murtaugh's Irish temper could have gotten the best of him. However, the feisty manager was one person who never backed away from a challenge. Instead of chastising the questioner, Murtaugh simply looked the reporter in the eye and responded in a soft voice, "I

Rennie Stennett—along with three other teammates on the '79 team—made history in 1971 when they became   part of the first ever starting lineup to feature all African-American players.

put the best nine athletes out there. The best nine I put out there tonight happened to be black. No big deal. Next question."

AMONG THE BEST IN A HUNDRED YEARS

ON SEPTEMBER 18, 1999, two players of the '79 Bucs, were named as members of the Pirates' "Team of the Century." Willie Stargell clearly outdistanced runner-up Dick Stuart as the first baseman in more than 14,000 votes cast by fans. Edging out ElRoy Face by slightly over 100 votes was Kent Tekulve as the team's relief specialist.

Other members of the honored squad included Bill Mazeroski (second base), Honus Wagner (shortstop), Pie Traynor (third base), Ralph Kiner (left field), Lloyd Waner (center field), Roberto Clemente (right field), Vernon Law (right-handed pitcher), Harvey Haddix (left-handed pitcher) and Danny Murtaugh (manager).

NOW THAT'S TIMELY

WHEN WILLIE STARGELL smashed a home run in the sixth inning of Game 7 of the 1979 World Series, he put the Pirates ahead by a score of 2-1. The Bucs would never relinquish that lead.

Stargell also had the honor of scoring the winning run in Game 7 of the 1971 Series as well. He scored the team's second (and deciding) run from first on an eighth-inning hit-and-run double off the bat of third baseman Jose Pagan as the Pirates upset another Baltimore team by winning the final contest, 2-1.

With Willie's homer in the last game of the '79 season it marked the first time in World Series history that one player scored the winning run in Game 7 for two world championship teams.

YOU CAN'T GET ANY BETTER THAN THIS

ANSWER THIS QUICKLY. Who was the player with the highest batting average during the regular season for the world champion Pittsburgh Pirates in 1979? Willie Stargell? No. He hit .281. Dave Parker? He hit .310. Bill Madlock? Among the regulars, he had the highest average—.328. It may surprise you to learn that the highest batting average belonged to a pitcher—Rick Rhoden.

Rhoden, who appeared in only one game in '79 and pitched a total of five innings, had one official at-bat on May 8 and laced a single off pitcher Eddie Solomon of the Atlanta Braves at Fulton County Stadium.

Rhoden left the Bucs' roster early in the season because of shoulder problems and had surgery on June 28, ending his season.

His short tenure with the team that year notwithstanding, Rick Rhoden became one of the few men in major league baseball who can boast that he ended the season with the highest possible batting average of 1.000.

THE AMAZING TEKULVE

HERE ARE SOME interesting statistics about ace reliever Kent Tekulve:

• In 1,050 games that spanned 16 major league seasons, he never once started a game as a pitcher.

• In 1979, he had a career-high and a league-leading 91 appearances and posted a career-high 31 saves.

• In the World Series, reliever Kent Tekulve appeared in five of the seven games, pitched 9.1 innings, gave up only four hits and three walks, while striking out ten and collecting three saves.

• Counting the games in the postseason, Tekulve appeared in 101 games for the Bucs in 1979.

THE BEST ARM SINCE CLEMENTE

PIRATE FAITHFUL WHO saw Dave Parker play in 1979 knew that their right-fielder had the best throwing arm in all of baseball. Many say he had the best arm since Roberto Clemente guarded the territory.

Parker opened the eyes of the nation to this fact during the All-Star Game that year at the Seattle Kingdome. In fact, he was named the MVP of the game chiefly because of two memorable throws from right field in Seattle's Kingdome that helped to preserve a 7-6 victory for the National League.

PRESSURE

PRIOR TO THE TEAM going onto the field for a nationally televised game on ABC, Willie Stargell was waiting in the dugout, where he was approached by Howard Cosell. The legendary lawyer-turned-sportscaster delighted in challenging athletes to answer philosophical questions that may or may not have had anything to do with the game. Most ballplayers responded to Cosell's questions with a look akin to a deer at night staring into the headlights of a car. Not Willie Stargell, as evidenced by his answer on this particular afternoon. Thrusting a microphone in front of the Pirates' star first baseman, Cosell posed a question in a tone that emulated a prosecuting attorney examining a murder suspect in court: "Willie, don't you find yourself succumbing to the immense pressure of leading your team onto the field of play during big game like this?"

"Pressure?" answered a calm, reserved Stargell. "That's not real pressure. Pressure is having five kids and two jobs and just trying to put food on the table."

Stargell's honest and real-world reasoning muzzled the normally verbose Cosell, who could add nothing to enhance the exchange.

WILLIE STARGELL AND FORBES FIELD

FORBES FIELD, HOME of the Bucs from June 30, 1909 to June 28, 1970, was one of the biggest ballparks in the major leagues. Measuring 365 feet down the left-field line, 457 feet in left-center, 435 feet in center, 375 feet in right center and 300 feet down the right-field line with an 18-foot wire fence above 9.5 feet of concrete, it was one of the most difficult venues in which to hit home runs. This didn't seem to phase Willie Stargell too much; some of his home-run blasts would have left any park, including Yellowstone. Of the 475 homers he hit in his career, seven of them went over the right-field roof at Forbes Field. To put this feat into proper perspective, a total of 18 were hit over that roof by the thousands of players who appeared there in uniform during the 60-year history of the ballpark.

In 1969, the last full season at Forbes Field, Stargell slugged 29 home runs. By comparison, in his first full season at Three Rivers Stadium, he hit 48 four-baggers. Stargell's wife at the time, Dolores, kept detailed statistics on every ball that her husband had hit and estimated that he would have hit 22 more home runs in '69 had the Pirates played in Three Rivers Stadium that year.

KISS IT GOODBYE!

MS. SALLY O'LEARY, a longtime, faithful member of the Pirates' front office, wrote in the players' alumni magazine about the last day of the home of the 1979 world champion Pirates.

"It was a beautiful sunny morning, 21-degree temperatures, on Sunday, February 11, 2001. In just 19 seconds on that morning, Three Rivers Stadium became a pile of rubber and dust at 7:59 a.m.

"More than 20,000 people viewed the blast from Point State Park; several thousand more were on Mount Washington. Others were scattered in downtown skyscrapers, on boats at the confluence of the Ohio, Monongahela and Allegheny, and in other locations to bid adieu to the stadium that had brought so many highs and lows in Pirate history since 1970.

"More than 4,800 pounds of dynamite in 2,500 locations in the stadium were needed to bring down the tons of structural steel and reinforcing bars.

"It was a festive atmosphere with helicopters and blimps circling around, vendors selling t-shirts and fans throwing parties. Yet it was bittersweet in many ways, with so many memories coming to mind of the great home runs, the championships, the no-hitters, the tough losses and the close victories over the years.

"By opening day at PNC Park, the entire area was cleared of the rubble, and it's hard to believe that a structure of this size actually stood in that area. However, those of us who spent a good deal of our lifetime at Three Rivers will always treasure the good days at this proud structure and will carry our memories right along with us to our new ballpark where we can compile a whole new list of things to remember and cherish.

"As our friend, Bob Prince, said many times, 'Kiss it Goodbye!'"

EPILOGUE

"If you can't play for Chuck Tanner, you can't play for anybody."

—All 25 players of the 1979
World Champion Pittsburgh Pirates

Celebrate the Heroes of Pittsburgh and Pennsylvania Sports with these Other Great Titles from Sports Publishing!

Tales from the Pirates Dugout
by John McCollister

- 5.5 x 8.25 hardcover
- ISBN: 1-58261-630-2
- 200 pages
- photos throughout
- $19.95

The Pittsburgh Pirates Encyclopedia
by David Finoli and Bill Ranier

- 8.5 x 11 hardcover
- ISBN: 1-58261-416-4
- photos throughout
- 400 pages • $39.95

Roethlisberger: Pittsburgh's Own Big Ben
by Sports Publishing L.L.C.

- 8.5 x 11 trade paper
- 128 pages
- color photos throughout
- $14.95
- 2005 release!

Tales from Behind the Steel Curtain
by Jim Wexell

- 5.5 x 8.25 hardcover
- ISBN: 1-58261-536-5
- 200 pages
- photos throughout
- $19.95
- 2004 release!

Myron Cope: Double Yoi!
by Myron Cope

- 6 x 9 hardcover
- ISBN: 1-58261-548-9
- 300 pages
- 8-page photo insert
- $22.95

Andy Russell: A Steeler Odyseey
by Andy Russell

- 6 x 9 limited-edition leatherbound
- ISBN: 1-58261-595-0
- 8-page b/w photo insert
- 272 pages • $149.95
- Signed by Andy Russell, Jack Ham, Jack Lambert, Rocky Bleier, Joe Greene, and Mel Blount!

Tales from the Pitt Panthers
by Sam Sciullo Jr.

- 5.5 x 8.25 hardcover
- ISBN: 1-58261-198-x
- 200 pages
- photos throughout
- $19.95
- 2004 release!

Roberto Clemente: The Great One
by Bruce Markusen

- 6 x 9 softcover
- 362 pages
- 12-page photo insert
- $16.95

Legends of the Philadelphia Phillies
by Robert Gordon

- 8.5 x 11 hardcover
- 160 pages
- photos throughout
- $24.95
- 2005 release!

Richie Ashburn Remembered
by Fran Zimniuch

- 8.5 x 11 hardcover
- 160 pages
- photos throughout
- $19.95
- 2005 release!

Available at Bookstores Everywhere!
Or to order at any time, please call toll-free **877-424-BOOK (2665)**.
For fast service and quick delivery, order on-line at **www.SportsPublishingLLC.com**.